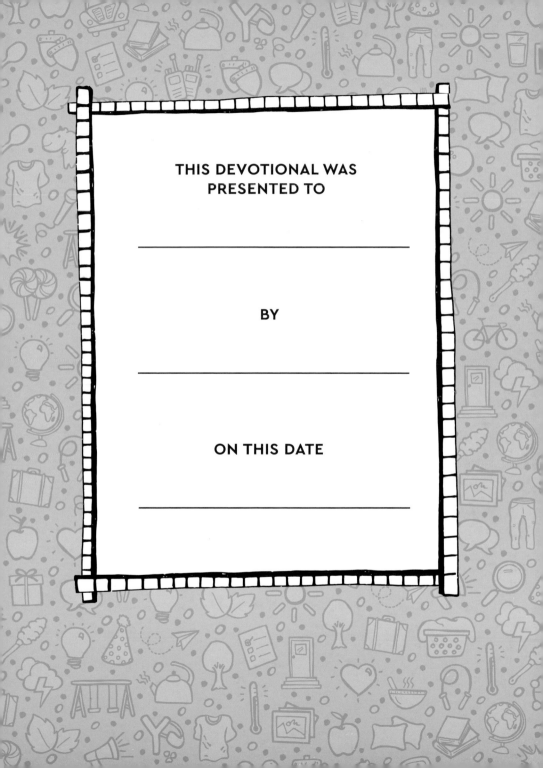

THIS DEVOTIONAL WAS
PRESENTED TO

_____

BY

_____

ON THIS DATE

_____

101 Parent/Kid Devotions to Experience the Adventure of Living Life with God

JOYCE MEYER

Printed in the United States of America.

First Printing, 2019

ISBN: 978-1-942854-94-4

Joyce Meyer Ministries
P.O. Box 655
Fenton, Missouri 63026
joycemeyer.org

As a mother, grandmother and great-grandmother, I understand the pressure of directing little hearts toward Christ and wanting to be a good parent. In fact, there have been countless moments where I've thought, *Joyce, you're just not good enough and you are going to mess these kids up!* But here's something God spoke to me that I want to share with you: You're not perfect. You may be weak, but it's in your weakness that He is strong.

He's given you all the grace you need to raise your children! So, don't give in to the temptation to think you can't do it. Trust me, I've been around that mountain too many times to recall and it only robs you and your family of your time and joy!

I truly believe that as we do our best, as we rely on God for everything—including raising our kids—God will take care of the rest. I've said it before and it's worth saying again: If we do what we feel God is asking us to do, He will take care of the rest. So, cut yourself some slack today! God's got them… and YOU.

Now, as a parent, caretaker or mentor, there is a great joy in seeing the children in your world enjoying life. You want to see them have the **best day ever**! But you know what that means? It means that they understand that there is a battle happening in their minds. Your prayer is that they can face fear and have the confidence in Christ to do it afraid. In a world that tells them to be selfish—to only ask the question *what about me*—you're looking to shape and guide them to be keenly aware of the needs of those around them. And most importantly, you want to hear them confessing the Word out loud in their own lives each day and be equipped to face a shaky world, firmly rooted in Him.

I wholeheartedly believe what I'm about to tell you: *If you teach a child the importance of following God's Word, you are less likely to have to fix an adult.*

These truths never change, but the world and culture do. So, I asked our youngest son, Daniel, and his wife, Nicol, what they would want to say to other parents, what their hopes and prayers are for those reading these words. And here's what they had to say...

> *Growing up, my mom was always reading her Bible. So even as a little kid, I figured there was something special about the Word. We knew not to talk to mom until she had spent time with God and had her coffee. The four of us kids knew this was a really vital part of the day.*
>
> *For our entire lives, she has imparted to us the impor-tance of studying the Word of God. Watching her study and seeing how God was working in her and changing her was so cool to be a part of. Now as a dad, I can't imagine not doing the same for my kids.*
>
> *My wife and I want our kids to know that no matter what they experience in life, they were created in Christ and have been called to do big things for Him. We want them to know, that even on their hardest day, the*

*Creator of the universe loves them! And that with His help, every day can be the **best day ever**. That's awesome!*

The opportunity to talk about God together as a family is so important to us, and the more we can incorporate God into our boys' daily lives, the more it's going to stick as they continue to grow.

That's why I am looking forward to using this devotional with them. It's a great tool for us to have conversations with them about who God is and how He is a part of everything we do. How He is the one that helps us to have the best day ever. I hope you enjoy it as much as we do!

Daniel & Nicol Meyer

We all want our kids to be happy...and the first step is leading them toward Christ and making **the choice** to have the **best day ever**. And spending time with God each day is a part of that choice. I pray that as you both make this choice together, You **and** your child will be transformed by the power of God's Word. I pray that your kids will know God is always on their side and that His Words are the ones that truly make a difference.

I LOVE YOU SO MUCH,

Joyce Meyer

This is the moment where everything changes.

Where you make the choice to have the best day ever

and see it happen before your eyes...

DAY 1

READY, GET SET... GO!

...I came that they may have and enjoy life,
and have it in abundance....
John 10:10 (AMP)

Ready to have the ***best day ever***? Well, the first step in having that best day is to *decide* that it's going to be the ***best day ever***. It won't happen on its own and you won't accidentally step into it.

So right now, this very moment, the best thing you can do is take a few minutes to stop and think about what kind of day you **want** to have. Do you **want** to laugh a lot, get along with friends, easily understand what you're being taught? Of course you do! I know I do!

Your thoughts are important. Your thoughts are where every single thing you'll do today begins. If you wake up a little grumpy and don't think about how to change that grumpiness for gratitude, all day you will likely feel grumpy.

But you might be thinking: **How do I change how I feel?** And that's a fantastic question! It's true, you may not be able to change how you feel right away, but you **can** start thinking about the things that make you feel differently.

So, when you start to *think* like Jesus, you'll also start to say things Jesus would say—and that's what makes any day better! I say it like this: *In your journey with Jesus, your worst day with Him will always be better than your best day without Him!* So...you are not only going to have just *another* day at school, but you're going to have the **best day ever**.

KID PRAYER

God, thank You for today. Help me to represent You well. Let me say the words You would say and treat everyone with kindness because they are important and matter.

PARENT PRAYER

God, help me to not get overly distracted with the cares of being an adult, and remember to enjoy life with my kids— not just endure it!

RISE + SHINE

In the morning, Lord, you hear my voice;
in the morning I lay my requests before you
and wait expectantly.
Psalm 5:3 (NIV)

Some days, morning comes too early! You know you have to get out of bed but you just don't want to. You want to sleep. You want **five more minutes**. You want to pull the covers over your head and hide. But why hide? The fact that you woke up this morning is a miracle! God put breath in your lungs and you have been given that breath to go about your day as best as you can. Think about all the incredible things you'll accomplish today!

In fact, every single day is another day for something amazing to happen. You just have to expect it to happen. Ask God to not only show you something amazing, but to do something amazing through you. So, before I get up every morning, I say it like this: "Something good is going to happen to me, and something good is going to happen through me today!"

KID PRAYER

. . . .

God, help me today. Show me something new, something amazing (neat clouds in the sky, a kind word spoken at school). Help me to be grateful for my family and friends and let me be kind to those around me—even if they don't know You.

PARENT PRAYER

. . . .

God, from the start of each day, I will be honest and sincere about my love for You and my love for my children. Then, I will release them into Your very capable care.

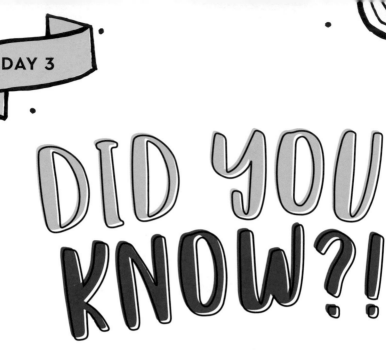

DID YOU KNOW?!

This God—his way is perfect;
the word of the Lord proves true;
he is a shield for all those who take refuge in him.
Psalm 18:30

Did you know that God is perfect, and He protects you?
Woah. That's a pretty big statement! Have you ever tried to be perfect, or at least, go one or two days without doing anything wrong? Without saying anything unkind or being mean to your little brother or sister? You see! It's impossible. Whether it's something big or small, here's the bottom line: You aren't perfect...and neither is anyone else in your life.

BUT, again, there **is** Someone who is perfect—and that person is God! His words are perfect, His ways are perfect (which means *there isn't a single thing He does that isn't perfect*), and His plans for your life are perfect!

And because you belong to Him—because you are one of His kids—He watches over you and protects you. Like an enormous shield, God has you covered, and He will never stop saving you from harm.

KID PRAYER

God, thank You for being perfect in all Your ways and always having my best interests in mind.

PARENT PRAYER

God, I know You love me and I ask You to protect my children and help me to do a good job parenting them.

FERRIS WHEEL

**It is the Lord who goes before you.
He will be with you; he will not leave you or forsake you.
Do not fear or be dismayed.**
Deuteronomy 31:8

• •

You've been waiting all week to go to the carnival in the parking lot! You drive by it every morning on your way to school. And for a whole week, you've watched all the lights and movement of the rides pass by outside the window on your way home. You begged your mom and dad to take you, and today is the day!

When you get there, when you get out of the car and walk to the front gates, directly in front of you is a giant Ferris wheel! Like **GIANT!** You think to yourself, *Ummm, it didn't look that*

big from my car window! And just like that, you move from excitement to fear.

Fear can happen at any moment and for any reason. And though you've been daydreaming about riding the Ferris wheel, now you are second-guessing yourself. You are being confronted (which means *it's right in your face*) by the fear of it, and you have to make a decision. Do you overcome your fears and get in line? Or do you let the feelings of fear keep you off the wheel?

Here's a great little secret to know: Just because you feel fear doesn't mean you can't face fear. I've found this little saying is helpful to learn and say out loud: "Even if I feel afraid... that's okay—I'll do it afraid!" Remember, God will help you in every single situation, big or small. Teeny tiny to the big ol' Ferris wheel standing before you. Fear might feel big, but God is bigger.

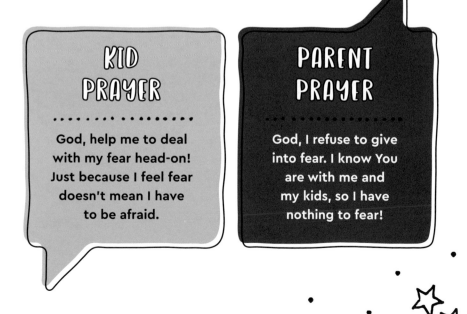

KID PRAYER

God, help me to deal with my fear head-on! Just because I feel fear doesn't mean I have to be afraid.

PARENT PRAYER

God, I refuse to give into fear. I know You are with me and my kids, so I have nothing to fear!

DAY 5

BEST. SCHOOL YEAR. EVER.

Say to those with an anxious and panic-stricken heart,
"Be strong, fear not! Indeed, your God will come
with vengeance [for the ungodly]; The retribution
of God will come, But He will save you."
Isaiah 35:4 (AMP)

Listen! If you want to have the best school year ever, you have to believe God will help you have it! That's right! God is going to help you learn, He is going to make sure you have all the friends you need, and He is going to help you every day. That's how much God cares for you.

Now, here's the thing though...it doesn't mean every day at school is going to be great. You might even have some tough days. You might forget to study for a quiz and get a

bad grade. You might have a disagreement with one of your best friends and now you are angry at each other. But the good news is those are just moments (accidents even). They are not who you are!

God's Word promises that He will always be with you. So, if you find yourself going through something difficult at school, don't be so quick to get on the phone with your friend, but instead, go right to God with it. He is interested in every single moment of your life! All you have to do is make it your daily goal to always get Him in to the mix of your life.

KID PRAYER

. . . .

God, I can't control what happens every day, but I can trust You every day to take care of me. Help me to rely on You—no matter what the day looks like.

PARENT PRAYER

. . . .

God, when I feel alone or like I'm missing the mark as a parent, help me to make the choice to trust You and Your Word.

OUR GOD IS GREATER!

A giant nearly ten feet tall stepped out from the Philistine line into the open, Goliath from Gath. He had a bronze helmet on his head and was dressed in armor—126 pounds of it! He wore bronze shin guards and carried a bronze sword. His spear was like a fence rail—the spear tip alone weighed over fifteen pounds. His shield bearer walked ahead of him.

1 Samuel 17: 4-7 (MSG)

• • • • • • • • • • • • • • • • • • • •

Have you read the story of David and Goliath? David is this very small kid—around the age of 13—and he ends up having to fight this big bully giant named Goliath. If you read the story itself in 1 Samuel 17, you'll notice that Goliath was so scary that no one wanted to fight him. But here's the really important part—David had God on his side. Yep. It's true.

Even though everything around David looked like he was going to lose the fight, he ended up winning it.

The reason? Even though Goliath was big and scary, David loved God and knew He would help him win. And though you don't come across real giants anymore, you do still have giants in your life.

There's the giant of fear, the giant of not feeling good enough, the giant of anger. And these giants are very real. So, what do you do? What do you do if you find yourself staring down the face of fear? You say very boldly, "My God is greater than anything! And He will help me!"

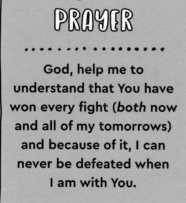

KID PRAYER

· · · · · · · · · · · · · ·

God, help me to understand that You have won every fight (*both* now and all of my tomorrows) and because of it, I can never be defeated when I am with You.

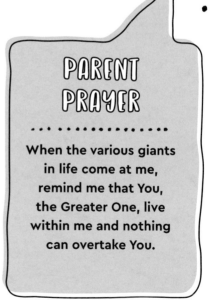

PARENT PRAYER

· · · · · · · · · · · · · · ·

When the various giants in life come at me, remind me that You, the Greater One, live within me and nothing can overtake You.

YOU KNOW YOU WANNA!

**Therefore the Lord waits [expectantly] and longs
to be gracious to you, and therefore He waits
on high to have compassion on you....**
Isaiah 30:18 (AMP)

Let's jump right in today. Say this out loud: "Something good is going to happen to me today." Yep. Put a big, cheesy smile on your face and say it again...and as loud as you can: **Something good is going to happen to me today**.

But...you have a doctor's appointment this afternoon, or a big test today or a tryout for the soccer team you really want to play on. Maybe you haven't even gotten out of bed yet and you're already worried, so you wonder why you should even start things off with a saying like that?!

Well, let's think about that for a minute. When you said those words really loudly, how did it make you feel? Did you laugh a little? Did you feel something positive on the inside? If you didn't, try saying it again, but perhaps with a little more feeling and maybe even with a fun accent. Sometimes, if you want to change how you *feel* on the inside, you have to *say* some good stuff out loud—on the outside.

The reason? When you focus on God's words and make them your own, they will likely set you up for something good. Chew on that idea for a while.

KID PRAYER

God, help me be as excited about today as You are and let me look for Your goodness at every turn.

PARENT PRAYER

God, help me to slow down long enough so that I can allow Your patience and strength to restore me.

DECISIONS. DECISIONS. DECISIONS!

Teach me good judgment and knowledge,
for I believe in your commandments.
Psalm 119:66

· ·

You'll likely make a lot of decisions today. Your mom or dad may ask you what you want for lunch. Your friends may ask if you want to play tag or kickball. Or perhaps the decisions will be a little more serious. Your friends may ask you to help them cheat on a test. Someone might ask you to lie to your mom or dad.

These are all decisions. And whether big or small, serious or a little silly, God promises that He will help you make them. If you take the time to ask Him, He will help you make the best decisions for your life.

And here's the neat thing about God: *Your* good decisions may look a little different than your friends' good decisions. Because God has a very detailed plan for your life, you have to be confident in the decisions He has for you and not compare them with anyone else's. Don't be swayed (which means *being talked into something else*) by the crowd. Making God happy is the only thing that matters!

KID PRAYER

God, help me make good decisions that honor You. I cannot do it in my own strength!

PARENT PRAYER

God, help me to make good, godly decisions based on Your Word. I know in my own strength I will fall short, but in Your strength, You'll never let me down.

HIS LOVE FOR YOU GOES ON AND ON...

**God is our refuge and strength,
a very present help in trouble.**
Psalm 46:1

Are you dealing with something **really** tough today? Did you let someone down who you really care about? Maybe someone you love got sick and died. Maybe your family life looks different than before: Mom and Dad don't live in the same house anymore. The list could go on and on...but there is something else that goes on and on...

That is God's great and incredible love for you! Yep, you are at the very center of God's heart. There is not a single day or moment that God's love does not completely surround you (even during the bad ones).

And though there aren't always answers that make you feel better, you don't have to be afraid to trust and rely on God. He will never leave or abandon you. No matter what. No matter what tough stuff you are dealing with, God will always be there for you. You can feel safe in His arms. You can run to Him and tell Him anything you want. If you are hurting, tell God— you can even yell out as loud as you want to Him! He not only understands what you are going through, but He sent His Son, Jesus, to help you.

You are one incredible kid. Sure, life might send you a curveball or two, something may shock or take you by surprise, but remember that it's not a surprise to God. He can handle it all.

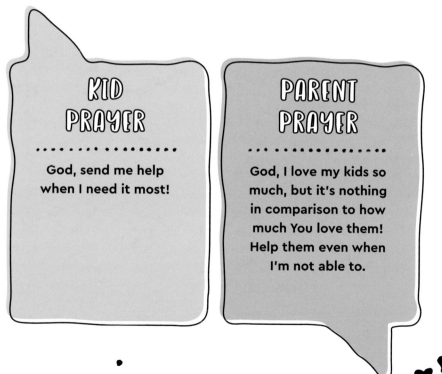

KID PRAYER

God, send me help when I need it most!

PARENT PRAYER

God, I love my kids so much, but it's nothing in comparison to how much You love them! Help them even when I'm not able to.

DAY 10

SUPERHERO STATUS

**He gives strength to the weary
and increases the power of the weak.**
Isaiah 40:29 (NIV)

· ·

You may not feel superhero-strong, but God gives you the strength you need every day. And don't worry about being strong tomorrow! He gives you what you need, at the very moment you need it. Which, if you think about it, really takes the pressure off!

And today, if you woke up feeling weak or worrying about something that's happening today, or if you are going to bed nervous about tomorrow, stop right where you are. That's

right. Stop and take the next two minutes to breathe and ask God for help. In fact, during this time, say things out loud like, "I know I can do this—God said He'd help me," and even, "I don't have to worry—if I feel weak, that's OK! God's got me!"

I've learned that there's nothing better than peace! Studying and focusing on God's Word is what fuels your ability to have His strength. And with God's Word working in your life, it gives you the boost you need to take on anything!

KID PRAYER

. . . .

God, when I feel weak or totally drained, please send me Your strength.

PARENT PRAYER

. . . .

God, I refuse to focus on my weaknesses because I know You send Your strength to me. You are faithful and always come to my rescue.

DAY 11

I DON'T FEEL GOOD

He sent out his word and healed them....
Psalm 107:20

Have you ever gotten up in the middle of the night with a bellyache? Has it ever been more serious, and you had to go to the doctor first thing in the morning to get the medicine you need to help you feel better? Well, just like in life, the best way to feel better is to read and take in the words of the Bible just like you would medicine. No matter what you're going through or how you feel, the Bible is there to help!

You can trust that God loves you and know that His Word (the Bible) is always there to lead and guide you! When you don't feel well or you are having a hard day, it can be as simple as saying, "God, I know you love me and that you are taking care of me, and it's going to get better. You are working in me right now." Then pull out your Bible and learn about how He's always there to take care of you!

And then once you feel better, or your day gets better, it's a great idea to find someone else who doesn't feel well or is having a bad day and encourage them! *Doing good* is a great next step once you've learned to trust God with every situation.

KID PRAYER

. . . .

God, I am going to trust You. No matter what happens today, I know that You love me and are taking care of me.

PARENT PRAYER

. . . .

God, help me to trust every word You speak— especially concerning my children—and I will do my best to help them develop the good life You have set aside for them.

MY LAUNDRY BASKET EXPLODED!

For each will have to bear his own load.
Galatians 6:5

Doing the right thing doesn't just involve all the big stuff in your life. In fact, if you do the little things right **now**, you won't have to clean up big messes **later.** For example, think about your laundry basket. Have you ever made a game out of balancing one more sock or T-shirt on the pile? And rather than take the super-full basket downstairs to get the clothes washed, you just keep stacking and stacking.

But then one day, you're running a little late to get to your baseball game. You are searching everywhere for your socks. You look in your drawers—and nothing! As you are about to

run downstairs to ask your mom, you look over and see the piece of artwork that's been created by smelly old clothes.

And once you dump all the clothes out, you do indeed find your socks at the bottom, and they smell terrible! But here's the problem: You don't have any time to do anything about it. You've got to go—your mom is calling you from the front door!

Though it's a silly example, if you would have done the right thing and taken care of your laundry basket earlier in the week, you wouldn't be in this sticky situation. You'd be on your way to win that game—and **not** with smelly socks! So, decide today that you will make the right choice right away.

KID PRAYER

God, help me to get the small things right—every single day, little by little— so when the big things come, I know what to do!

PARENT PRAYER

As a parent, I know it's the little things that can rob me of my joy. So today, God, help me with the little stuff so I can keep moving forward.

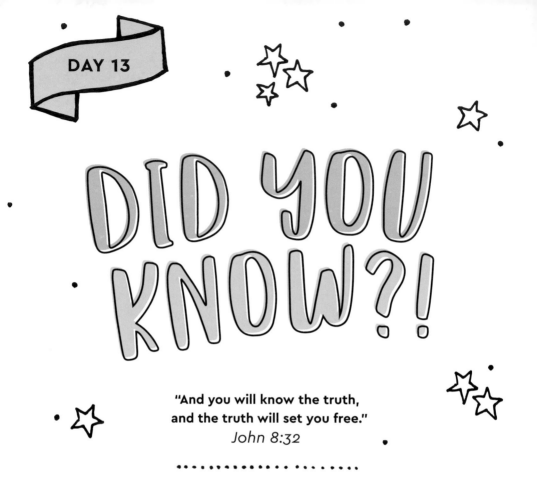

DID YOU KNOW?!

"And you will know the truth,
and the truth will set you free."
John 8:32

· · · · · · · · · · · · · · · · · · · ·

Did you know that you can understand God's Word for yourself? That you aren't too small or young or anything like that! God promises that if you read the Bible and do your best to follow it, He will always be with you and will always help you.

And perhaps you are curious about the last few words in to-day's scripture? *Set you free?* What exactly does that mean? Well, you may remember learning about Adam and Eve—the whole apple-in-the-garden business. When they made the decision to disobey and eat the fruit God told them not to,

they got in trouble. BIG trouble. Have you ever been in a situation like that with your mom or dad?

You do something they've told you not to and you get in trouble and have to deal with the consequences (which really just means *the outcomes of your actions*). Maybe you even get grounded and aren't allowed to do anything for a week!

And while you are in trouble, you feel trapped inside the house—like a prisoner! But when you've proven to your mom or dad you understand what you did wrong—when you follow their words and are willing to obey them—you hear the words you've been waiting for: "OKAY! You've learned your lesson! You are free to go outside and play!"

The same is true with God: When you follow God's Word like you would an instruction book, you are free to live life to the max!

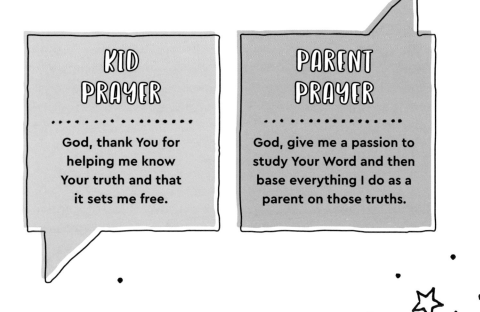

KID PRAYER

God, thank You for helping me know Your truth and that it sets me free.

PARENT PRAYER

God, give me a passion to study Your Word and then base everything I do as a parent on those truths.

TWO POWERFUL WORDS

If we confess our sins, he is faithful and just to forgive us our sins and to cleanse us from all unrighteousness.
1 John 1:9

. . . .

Do you know what two of the most powerful words are? You've likely said hundreds of things already today, but you may not have said **these** two words yet. In fact, no matter how old you are, these can be the two hardest words to say. Both young and old have a hard time saying them...so here we go, let's just say them out loud: **"I'm sorry."**

Yep. **Those** two words. When you say you're sorry, it means you didn't act in the right way. You said something hurtful when you were mad. You feel terrible for what you did, but you also don't like feeling this way—it's no fun at all! So, instead of being quick to apologize, you distract yourself with other stuff.

But ignoring something doesn't make it go away, and it can actually make things worse! You made a mistake and the right thing to do—the **best thing** to do—is to say, "I'm sorry. I made a mistake. Can you forgive me?" The neat thing about that is when people see that you mean it, they are quick to forgive you.

Today, if you make a mistake, be quick to apologize (which means *saying **"I'm sorry"***) and then be quick to move on with your life! There's no use feeling guilty over something that happened in the past if you've done all you can to make it right.

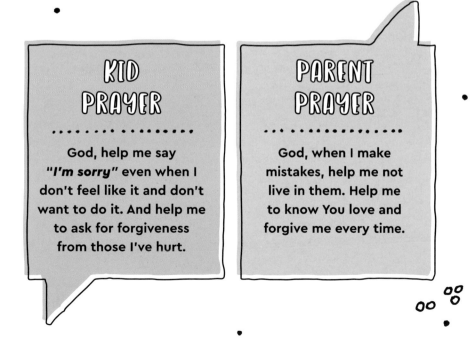

KID PRAYER

. . . .

God, help me say *"I'm sorry"* even when I don't feel like it and don't want to do it. And help me to ask for forgiveness from those I've hurt.

PARENT PRAYER

. . . .

God, when I make mistakes, help me not live in them. Help me to know You love and forgive me every time.

STORE IT UP!

**I have stored up your word in my heart,
that I might not sin against you.**
Psalm 119:11

If you've never watched a squirrel or chipmunk gather acorns, you are missing a really fun sight! They run around, looking for more and more acorns to collect. And the reason? They are collecting food now to have later once winter sets in. They prepare today for what is coming tomorrow.

God's Word is very similar. Sure, you don't know everything that's going to happen today. You're not 100 percent sure about what's going to happen tomorrow. But one thing

that's certain is this: You will need the help of His Word. And when you take the time (like you are doing right now) to study the Bible, and ask God to help you at the beginning of your day, you store up more and more of the help you'll need.

In other words, getting ready now is super-helpful for tomorrow. And when tomorrow comes, you won't have to run around, all confused. You can be confident because no matter what comes your way, you have plenty of God's Word ready to go inside of you, and you will make better choices because of it!

KID PRAYER

God, help me to fill up on Your Word now so that later on I'll know what to say and do!

PARENT PRAYER

God, I will store up a great surplus of Your Word, and when I find myself in a tough parenting moment, help me look to that surplus so I'll know what to do.

SUPER-DUPER EXTRA SOUR CANDY!

**Children, obey your parents in everything,
for this pleases the Lord.**
Colossians 3:20

The Bible has some pretty interesting things to say about honoring your parents. It says that if you do, it makes God happy. But what does honor look like? In what ways can you honor your parents? Even though honor sounds like a very serious word, it's actually not too hard.

You can honor, or respect, your parents by listening to them when they ask you to help with the dog. When they tell you to finish your homework and you get it done, it honors

them. When you want to do something really badly, but they tell you no...and you still have a good attitude—this **really** honors God.

But what is it like on the other side? When you *don't* do what they ask, when you *don't* keep your word with them, and when you *have* a bad attitude when you feel they've let you down? Well, it's like popping the most super-duper, extremely sour piece of candy into your mouth! Not the normal kind of sour—the overwhelming, can-hardly stand-it sour. Instead, be the sweet (maybe with a tiny-amount-of-good sour) kid who does their best to listen to their parents. Because at the end of the day, it's a great way to honor God.

KID PRAYER

God, help me to honor my parents even when I don't feel like it. I know that when I do, I'm really honoring You.

PARENT PRAYER

God, help me teach my kids what it looks like to honor and respect You as well as others with both my words and actions.

WANNA BUILD A FORT?

Your kingdom come, Your will be done, on earth as it is in heaven.
Matthew 6:10

• • • • • • • • • • • • • • • • • • • •

Do you ever build a fort with pillows, chairs and sheets? Maybe you even decorate it by bringing all your favorite stuff into it (games, pictures, music). You can build it high. You can build it under the stairs. But, wherever you like to build it, you are building a "little kingdom," because what you put inside of it is a reflection of you.

And though it doesn't work the same with pillows, chairs and sheets, every single day you get the awesome opportunity to build God's fort here on planet earth. Because God is the one true King, and because you love Him and He calls you one of His sons and daughters, you are **also** one of His "fort builders." When you choose not to gossip about a kid at school, when you say you are sorry to someone you've hurt, when you listen to what your parents say, or when you share your food with a friend who may not have any, you are building God's fort—His kingdom here on earth.

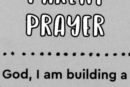

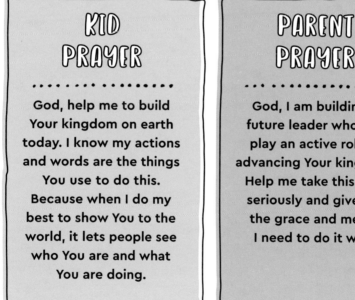

KID PRAYER

· · · · · · · · · · · · · ·

God, help me to build Your kingdom on earth today. I know my actions and words are the things You use to do this. Because when I do my best to show You to the world, it lets people see who You are and what You are doing.

PARENT PRAYER

· · · · · · · · · · · · · ·

God, I am building a future leader who will play an active role in advancing Your kingdom. Help me take this task seriously and give me the grace and mercy I need to do it well.

DAY 18

CHEER UP!

**This is my comfort in my affliction,
that Your word has revived me and given me life.**
Psalm 119:50 (AMP)

When you feel down, God will always find a way to cheer you up! And when you feel sad or upset because you've made a mistake, God is there to pick you up! Would you like to know why?

Because we serve a God who is very concerned for you, He doesn't want you to stay in that sad or guilty state! So, if you're feeling lonely, God wants to cheer you up! Read some of your favorite Bible verses to give you a boost. Or if you've done something bad, God wants you to ask for His forgiveness and move on! He doesn't want you to feel mopey.

Ask God to help you move forward. And the minute you do, you get a dose of both forgiveness and hope. And hope is the thing that gets you moving—it's the fuel that makes you feel refreshed and revived! So, today, if you feel like you're dragging, ask God to send His strength, hope and maybe even forgiveness your way.

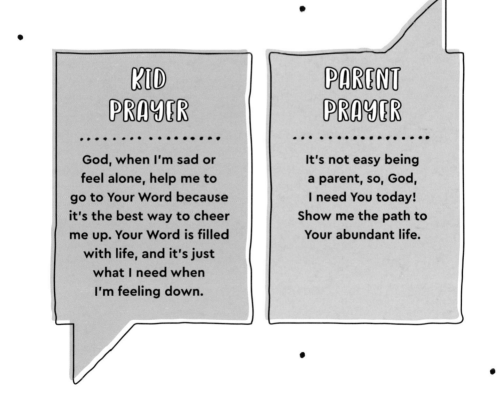

KID PRAYER

God, when I'm sad or feel alone, help me to go to Your Word because it's the best way to cheer me up. Your Word is filled with life, and it's just what I need when I'm feeling down.

PARENT PRAYER

It's not easy being a parent, so, God, I need You today! Show me the path to Your abundant life.

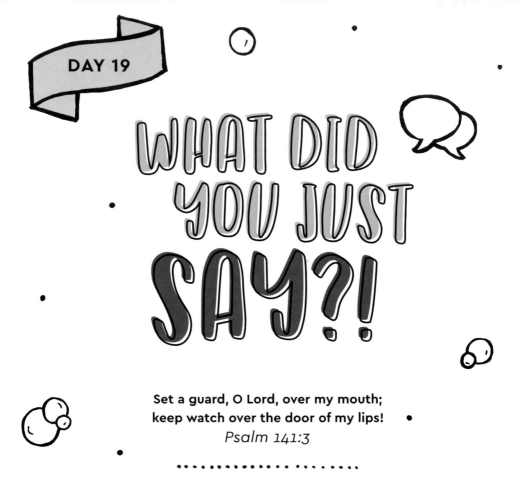

WHAT DID YOU JUST SAY?!

**Set a guard, O Lord, over my mouth;
keep watch over the door of my lips!**
Psalm 141:3

No, no, no! You're not in trouble, but it's probably a good time to do a quick mouth check. Wait? A mouth check? Well, you are reading these words with your mouth, so you know your mouth is still there...right? OK, your mouth is there, so what type of check is it?

Here you go. Think back over your day. What words did you use? Did you speak good words? Kind words? And though you've learned about the power of words before, let's look at one area in particular (which means *to focus right on it and nothing else*). What words did you use to talk about yourself?

Did you say today, "I'm stupid," or "I'm dumb"? Were you unkind to yourself? When taking a test, did you say out loud, "I'll probably get an F," or maybe even, "I'm terrible at everything"? How you talk about yourself is very important! In fact, do you think God thinks those things about you? Do you think God talks about you like that? Never! Over the years, God has taught me this incredible truth: *Words are containers for power!* What I say really matters!

Remember, more than anything else, He loves you. And it's time you start loving *you*, too! If you think you're not good enough, ask God to show you every day how much He loves you, and start replacing all those negative words with the truth of God's Word!

KID PRAYER

God, help me speak kind words about myself. Because I am Your kid, You don't like hearing me talk badly about myself.

PARENT PRAYER

God, please help me to stop wasting time speaking badly about myself or the way I parent my kids. I love You and Your Word, and I want to be a good example for my kids.

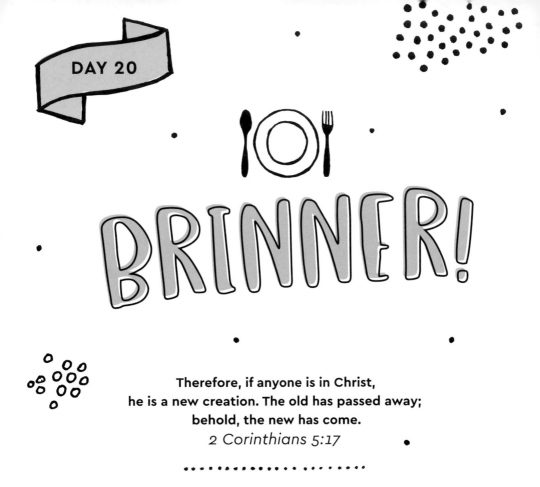

BRINNER!

Therefore, if anyone is in Christ,
he is a new creation. The old has passed away;
behold, the new has come.
2 Corinthians 5:17

If you don't know about the **amazing idea** that is breakfast for dinner, stop right now, turn to your parents and say, "**We must have BRINNER tonight!**" Now, of course, say that as sweet as possible and be sure to use the words, *"Please"* and *"I love you"* a lot, but breakfast for dinner is awesome! Even if you've never done it!

But just because something is different, it doesn't mean it isn't going to be great! That's the deal with new stuff. At first, you aren't sure if you will like it, but you should always give it a chance.

Think about it: You love breakfast! Sausage, hash browns, scrambled eggs with tons of cheese...toast...and let's not forget about **French toast** with maple syrup. Yum! So, are breakfast foods for dinner new? Yes. But does it **change** the fact that you love them? No!

The same is true in your life. Just because something is new, doesn't mean it's not going to be good. When you learned who Jesus was and you asked Him to live in your heart, He made you a new person. God took all the bad stuff away and your life changed for the better! So, you are new, too!

So, what does all this mean? It means no matter what happens today, be willing to try something new. Whether it's learning a new skill or making a friend at school, give it a try. You never know what cool new thing God has in store for you!

KID PRAYER

God, thank You for making me a new person. Thank You that I can get excited about trying new stuff!

PARENT PRAYER

God, give me the grace to be OK with who I am today, and the ability to learn new things that I'll need in the future.

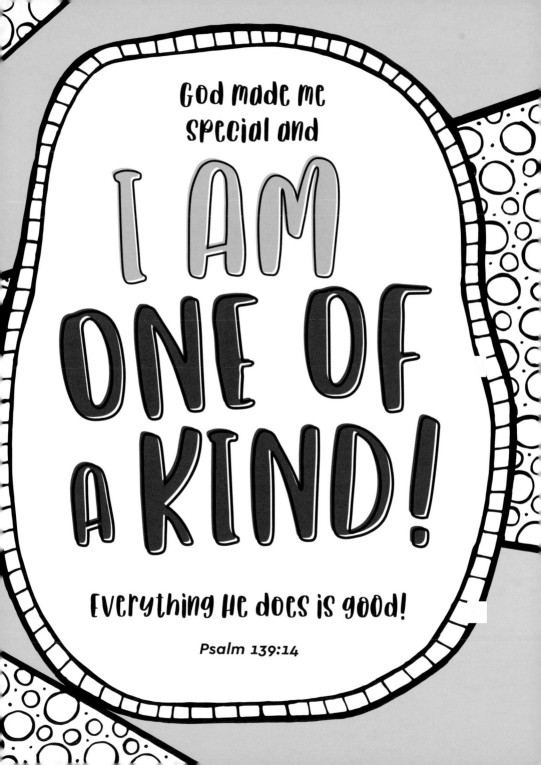

CRACK, SNAP + POP!

**Being strengthened with all power
according to his glorious might so that you
may have great endurance and patience.**
Colossians 1:11 (NIV)

On a cold and chilly Saturday morning, you get out of bed and your feet hit the floor. You think to yourself, *Oh my goodness! It's freezing in this house!* You creep out of your room, into the hallway and start down the steps. With each step on the stairs your feet get colder and colder.

When you come into the living room, much to your surprise and excitement, you see your parents building a fire—the first one of the year! Best of all, the fire is already going—the crack of the wood is like music to your ears, and the snap and pop of the embers tells you the house will warm up in a little while.

Sometimes in life, just like you have to wait to warm up by the fire, you may have to wait a little bit before your circumstances change. You have to be patient and you have to get through a little bit of discomfort before things turn around. And if you really want to get radical about waiting and being patient, try doing all those things with a smile on your face. Because here's the awesome truth: If you can be happy even when you are uncomfortable or don't get your way, you are growing in God and will learn to really enjoy life.

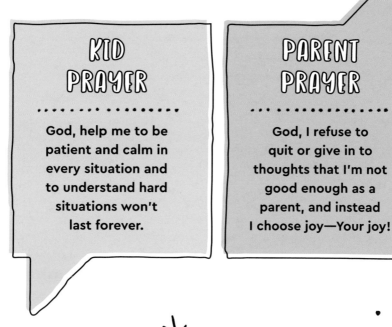

KID PRAYER

God, help me to be patient and calm in every situation and to understand hard situations won't last forever.

PARENT PRAYER

God, I refuse to quit or give in to thoughts that I'm not good enough as a parent, and instead I choose joy—Your joy!

CHICKEN FIGHT

**Finally, be strong in the Lord and in the
strength of his might.**
Ephesians 6:10

Summertime is one of the best times to be a kid. You get to run outside in the warm sun. You're off school and your friends are, too! The days are longer and the sun stays out forever! And because it's so hot, the pool is open.

And what happens in the pool? You splash, you chase each other around, and every once in a while you hop on your dad's shoulders and challenge another dad and friend to a game of chicken fight! The point of the game is to stay up longer on your dad's shoulders than your friend can and playfully knock them down.

Do you want to know a secret that will help you win the game? It's not so much about how strong you are but more about how strong your dad is! When you're on his shoulders, he can balance you using his stability in the pool, and he can make you even stronger because you are tapping into his strength. When you are "on" your dad's shoulders, you are even stronger "in" his strength.

And if your dad is king of the pool, think about how strong God is as King of the universe?! That's right. There's never a moment where God has lost anything. He is always in control!

KID PRAYER

God, I know I am my strongest when I am with You. Help me understand how powerful You are and that when I'm with You, I have access to Your might.

PARENT PRAYER

God, I don't have to be concerned about being strong in my own abilities, but instead, I realize that my strength comes from You.

PICTURE PERFECT?!

**So we have come to know and to believe the love
that God has for us. God is love, and whoever abides
in love abides in God, and God abides in him.**
1 John 4:16

Here's a little secret I'll let you in on. A picture is not real life. It may capture moments in time, but just because everything looks perfect, doesn't mean it always is! There are ways to edit the photo...in fact, you can take a photo that doesn't look that good and make it amazing with the right filter! But here's the thing: Just because something looks good on the outside doesn't mean it is on the inside. And whether it's social media, a picture in a magazine or on TV, those images aren't always real life—the way things *really* are!

And although pictures are not real life, the people inside the photos are. So, even if technology makes everything look perfect, it doesn't mean you have to pretend that you are. You are incredible—with no filter—just the way you are because God created you!

And when you decide to accept who you are (which really means *loving yourself the way God loves you*), you don't have to walk around pretending things are great all the time. Even on bad days, you can be honest with people and tell them you're having a rough day. But ultimately, you can know in your heart that God loves you and you aren't a surprise to Him. God made you just the way you are!

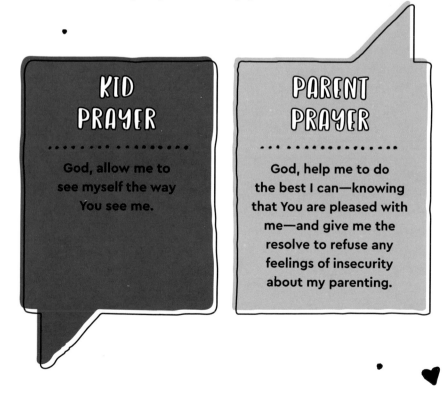

KID PRAYER

God, allow me to see myself the way You see me.

PARENT PRAYER

God, help me to do the best I can—knowing that You are pleased with me—and give me the resolve to refuse any feelings of insecurity about my parenting.

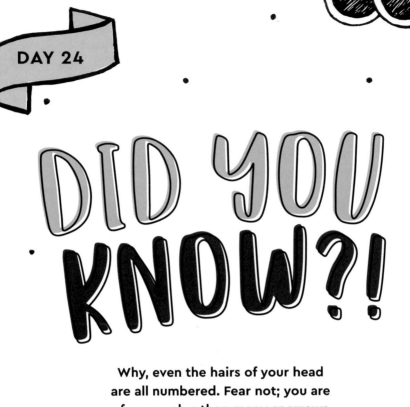

DID YOU KNOW?!

Why, even the hairs of your head are all numbered. Fear not; you are of more value than many sparrows.

Luke 12:7

Did you know that God knows the exact number of hairs on your head? Yep. It's true! And He knows how many hairs are always on your head! Even when your hair is extra crazy after a long night's sleep or when you are done with your shower and a couple fall out. Even after a haircut!

God knows everything about you, and He loves you like crazy! If you are concerned about something (which means *you can't stop thinking about it*), it's a concern to God and

He wants to help you with it! That's how important you are to Him!

And if God loves you and keeps such good watch over your life, you have nothing to fear! Think about it...the God of the universe, the God who has created every single person and everything you see around you, is on your side! He's like the best big brother ever (and an always-present Dad). The reason? You are super-valuable to Him and He has a great plan for your life.

KID PRAYER

God, it blows my mind that You know every single aspect about me. You will help me to not be afraid!

PARENT PRAYER

God, help me to stay peaceful and not give in to fear. Though I don't know how everything will play out in my kids' lives, I know You care for them and have a good plan.

SWINGS

**You shall give to him freely, and your heart
shall not be grudging when you give to him,
because for this the Lord your God will bless you
in all your work and in all that you undertake.**

Deuteronomy 15:10

• •

Do you love the swings at school? Or maybe the swing set
you have in your backyard? I'm not sure if you remember the
time you were learning how to swing on your own, but it
was hard work! You had to balance just right on the swing itself. You had to ask your parents for a push or two...and then,
THEN, you had to pump! It sounds like an easy thing, but it's
not easy at all! In fact, it's something you probably had to
work on for a while before you got it!

But hard work is important! Every time you do your best, every time you work really hard at something, you get better and better at it. All you have to do is stay at it. You don't need to get frustrated, and you don't have to be hard on yourself.

So, whatever you are working on today...maybe it's math, maybe it's learning how to swim in the deep end...or maybe it's being nice to your sister—never give up! Ask God to help you when things get hard and refuse to get mad or frustrated at yourself in the process.

KID PRAYER

God, help me to work hard and have a good attitude along the way.

PARENT PRAYER

God, allow me to demonstrate to my kids that life is an adventure. And sometimes that means learning something new—something that stretches me for the better!

DAY 26

WALKIE-TALKIE!

The eyes of the Lord are toward the righteous and his ears toward their cry.
Psalm 34:15

. . . .

Have you ever played with a *walkie-talkie?* Or maybe you've watched a movie where people are using them? Basically, they are a fun way for two people to communicate back and forth. But unlike a cell phone, there's a slight catch. The walkie-talkies work as long as they aren't super-far away from one another. How do you know you've gotten too far away? Words get cut off, the signal gets weak, and there is a lot of static. But the minute the two walkie-talkies are close together—they instantly work again! The signal is strong and words are crystal clear.

And once they are working great, you can start talking to your friend on the other end about anything. You might ask them their location. You might ask them if they know about the test coming up tomorrow at school. You might make plans to meet later at the park. Simply, you talk to them about anything!

The walkie-talkie is a great example of how you could look at prayer. Prayer doesn't have to be this very super-serious thing—you can talk to God at any time...and you don't even have to close your eyes! You just have to stay close to God, get Him in the mix of every situation of your life (AKA keep the signal strong), and then talk to Him like He's right there. But unlike a walkie-talkie, even when we feel far from God, He always hears us! *He's always right there on the other end.*

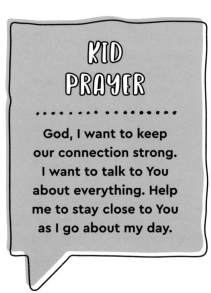

KID PRAYER

. . . .

God, I want to keep our connection strong. I want to talk to You about everything. Help me to stay close to You as I go about my day.

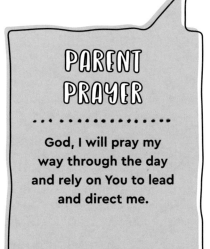

PARENT PRAYER

. . . .

God, I will pray my way through the day and rely on You to lead and direct me.

SNACK TIME IS THE BEST TIME

Give us this day our daily bread.
Matthew 6:11

Let's see if I can name some of your favorite snacks: animal crackers, yogurt, apples, potato chips, ice cream? Is at least one of those right? Now, pretend those snacks were your food for the **entire** day. You wouldn't need to worry about what you were going to eat because it was totally taken care of. You could giggle and tell everyone that you were eating cheese puffs all day!

Because God loves you, He's provided everything you need **for today**. You don't have to worry about tomorrow, next week, OR even next month! All you have to do is put a big smile on your face and know God is taking care of you **today**. Then, believe that just like today, God will be waiting for you tomorrow—and maybe tomorrow you'll get to have ice cream all day!

KID PRAYER

· · · · · · · · · · · · · · ·

God, give me what I need for today. Help me to not be worried or bothered by anything in the future. I know You are with me and will be with me all day giving me exactly what I need.

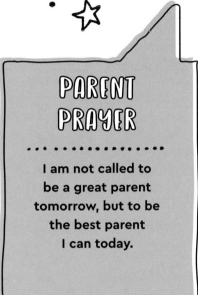

PARENT PRAYER

· · · · · · · · · · · · · · ·

I am not called to be a great parent tomorrow, but to be the best parent I can today.

PINKY PROMISE

**I have sought your face with all my heart;
be gracious to me according to your promise.**
Psalm 119:58 (NIV)

Have you ever done a *pinky swear?* Or said to your mom or dad, "I promise I'll do *this* or *that?"* And though you tried really hard to keep it, surely there's been a time or two where you've broken your promise.

Do you want to know something great? Though you may have accidentally broken a promise you made, God will not and cannot break any of His promises. So, if it's in God's Word, you can count on it to happen every time!

That means, when God says, "You will get mercy," you will absolutely get it! Every. Single. Time. We all need God's mercy. No matter who you are or what you've done, you just have to receive it (which is just another way to say *take it all in*).

And what is mercy? What does getting mercy look like? Well, I think about it like this: It's easy to give people what they deserve (like when someone says something mean and you say something even meaner back). But sharing mercy means being kind even though they were mean. Though it's hard to do, responding with mercy is always better! Sure, they may not deserve it, but if God does it for us, we should try really hard to do it, too!

KID PRAYER

God, thank You for the incredible promise of Your mercy!

PARENT PRAYER

God, help me get closer to You and to always rely on Your mercy.

DON'T BE AFRAID!

**The Lord is my light and my salvation; whom shall I fear?
The Lord is the stronghold of my life; of whom shall I be afraid?**
Psalm 27:1

Right now. Wherever you are reading these words, you need to know one thing: God is with you. Yep! It's true. Though you may not see Him or feel Him, He is by your side. That means you are never alone and have nothing to fear.

But, maybe you've gone through a situation where you were really afraid. You might have experienced something that scared you and it's been giving you bad dreams. And when nighttime comes, you really don't want to go to bed. You want to stay up—anything not to be alone.

But, remember, you are never alone—never, never, NEVER. Think about God like you do a best friend—one of your friends that you have tons of fun with! The laugh-so-hard-you-can't-even-stand type of giggling. The type of friend that you can tell anything to! A best friend who sticks up for you when people aren't kind and the type of friend where you can finish each other's sentences.

Got that type of friend in mind? OK, now add a million to that feeling, multiply it by a trillion...and then you might get close to the type of friend God is to you. So, yes, you may be afraid, you may have nightmares now and again, but remember Who is on your side—God!

And, as you lay in your bed, talk to God and ask Him to help you. Ask Him to protect your dreams and allow you to get good sleep! Sure, you may have to do it over and over again, but do not give up! God will help you overcome your fear!

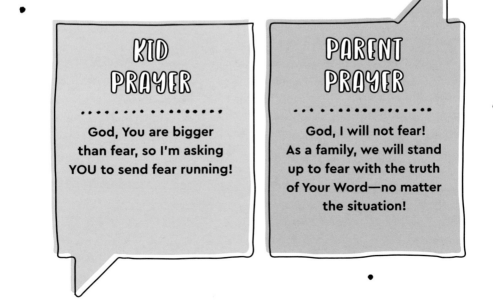

KID PRAYER

. . . .

God, You are bigger than fear, so I'm asking YOU to send fear running!

PARENT PRAYER

. . . .

God, I will not fear! As a family, we will stand up to fear with the truth of Your Word—no matter the situation!

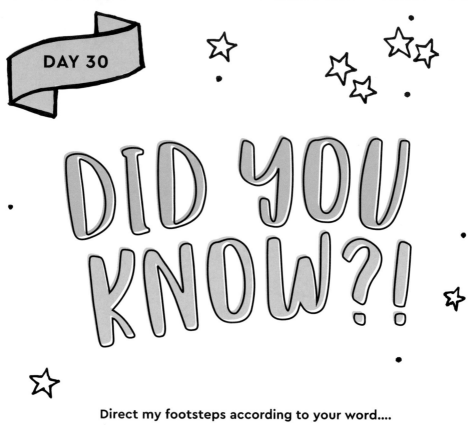

DID YOU KNOW?!

Direct my footsteps according to your word....
Psalm 119:133 (NIV)

• • • • • • • • • • • • • • • • • • • •

Did you know God already has all your steps planned? It's true! But you may be thinking, *How is that possible? How can God know exactly what I'll do?* And both are very good questions! Though God gives you the ability to make choices, He also has a plan for your life. From the beginning of time, He knew what your name would be, what family you'd be a part of, the friends you'd have—everything!

But even though God knows all those things, you still have to do your best to stay on God's path. He doesn't force you to stay on the trail. You can wander, you can stray, but when you do, the road becomes tough to walk on.

Asking God to help you stay on the right path makes the road *clearer*. It makes the road *easier* to travel because God has already planned your steps. Now, it doesn't mean tough things won't happen, but it does mean that God already saw them coming, and He already has a next step—a plan to help you out.

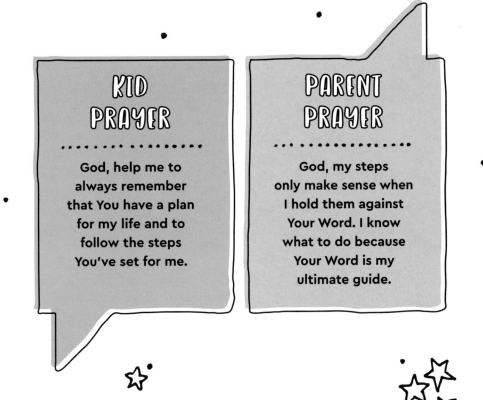

KID PRAYER

God, help me to always remember that You have a plan for my life and to follow the steps You've set for me.

PARENT PRAYER

God, my steps only make sense when I hold them against Your Word. I know what to do because Your Word is my ultimate guide.

I'm going to use all my energy, talents and skills for you!

1 Corinthians 10:31

GO AHEAD + JUMP!

You will keep in perfect peace those whose minds are steadfast, because they trust in you.
Isaiah 26:3 (NIV)

Maybe you've done this before: You stood six or seven steps higher than your mom and dad at the bottom of the steps and they yelled out to you, "Jump! I'll catch you!" Sure, at first you were a little scared and thought to yourself, *What if they don't catch me?* But once you did it and they were right there, you'd race back up the steps to do it again. What started as a scary thought ended up not being bad at all—in fact, it was really fun!

Just like this game, God is always going to be there to catch you—**always!** What you have to do sometimes is remind yourself of that. You have to make up your mind and *trust*, regardless of how it looks or how you feel about it. If you know God is calling you to jump, **jump!**

KID PRAYER

God, because I can trust You, help me to keep my mind free of doubt and worry. I want to have Your peace in every situation because I know how much You care for me. You love me and that means my life is going to be exciting!

PARENT PRAYER

God, sometimes I feel overwhelmed by the weight of raising my children. Help me to cast my cares and anxiety on You because I know You are taking good care of them.

FALLING LEAVES

**For everything there is a season, and a time
for every matter under heaven.**
Ecclesiastes 3:1

. . . .

Seasons change. Warm summer days start to turn cooler, fall arrives with the falling of the leaves. Soon after, the falling leaves are replaced with falling snow. And sure, winter has its moments of fun, but after a little while, when you are staring out the window, daydreaming of playing outside, the snow starts to melt and flowers pop up from the ground as spring emerges.

What do the seasons teach us? They show us that life is always moving and we are always growing. Imagine if winter would last all year?! Yikes and brrrrrrr...

God's Word says the earth needs all the various seasons, and so do you! You will have different seasons of your life. You may have friends this year who aren't your friends next year. You may be interested in playing sports this year and next year discover that you really like to play guitar or sing. You might hate brussels sprouts this year (and every year since you were little), and then all of a sudden, you start to actually like them! What?! It's true!

And here's the secret to changing seasons: You don't have to resist the changes, and you don't even have to feel bad about them or dread them. As long as you stay with God, He promises to help you move from season to season.

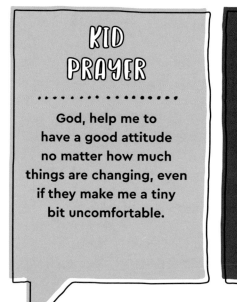

KID PRAYER

God, help me to have a good attitude no matter how much things are changing, even if they make me a tiny bit uncomfortable.

PARENT PRAYER

God, I won't fight against life changing. I will embrace it with tons of grace, knowing that if it's changing, You have already given me everything I need to deal with it.

THE REALLY REALLY KINDA LOVE

"For God so loved the world, that he gave his only Son, that whoever believes in him should not perish but have eternal life."

John 3:16

Guess what? God loves YOU! It sounds simple, sure, but God loves you. Like really, *really*, **really** loves you! He knows you make mistakes sometimes and still loves you. And are you ready for this? He not only knows who you are right now, but He knows who you will be tomorrow and when you are really old!

God loves you so much that His Son, Jesus, came to earth as a baby, grew up a lot like you did—learned how to walk, talk, eat, play...all the fun stuff—and then eventually when

He was much older, He went to the cross. And on that cross, when He died, He was thinking about you! And not the **you** when you are having a good day, listening to your parents and being kind to your siblings, but the you when **you** make mistakes, in the moments you are unkind and having the worst day ever!

Think about that! It's one thing to do something for someone who is being nice, but to do something incredible for a person who makes mistakes and is unkind is way different! And why did God do that? Why did Jesus go to the cross for you? It's simple: He loves you and thinks you are worth it. So, when you start to feel down in the dumps, or sad and lonely, just remember and say out loud: "I'm not perfect, but God still loves me!"

KID PRAYER

God, help me to understand more and more about how much You love me.

PARENT PRAYER

God, I will remind myself daily that You love me and You think I'm enough. The world is so tricky in making me feel less than, but I know You have great things in store for me.

GOD IS BIG + GREAT!

**And God said, "Let there be light,"
and there was light.**
Genesis 1:3

Let's try something fun today. Whether it's early in the morning or bedtime and dark outside, have your mom or dad stand by the light switch in the turned-off position and count down from 10. When they get to one, scream out loud, "Let there be light!" and have them flip the switch!

Ready? Give it a try. Maybe even give it three or four tries!

If you think that's cool, just imagine what it was like for God to turn on the lights for the entire ***everything of everything!***

And how did God do it? No, not with the flip of a switch, but instead with His Words and His power. That's right! God is so big and so powerful, that He can make a whole lot of something from *nothing*.

And He doesn't just create...no, no, no...He also keeps everything in the right place and makes sure that the planet continues to rotate, He keeps the clouds moving in the sky—everything! So, if you are worried about something, if you have a problem that you're not sure how to fix, remind yourself that God has all the answers...*and He cares about every single detail of your life.*

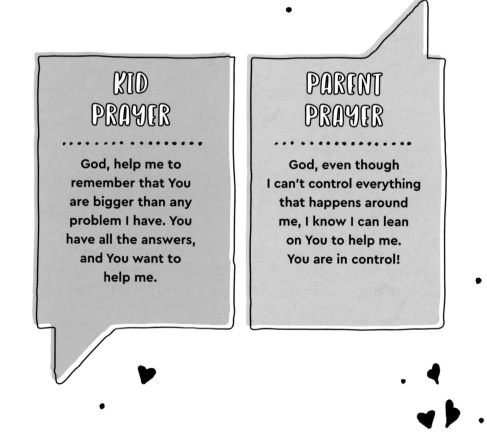

KID PRAYER

God, help me to remember that You are bigger than any problem I have. You have all the answers, and You want to help me.

PARENT PRAYER

God, even though I can't control everything that happens around me, I know I can lean on You to help me. You are in control!

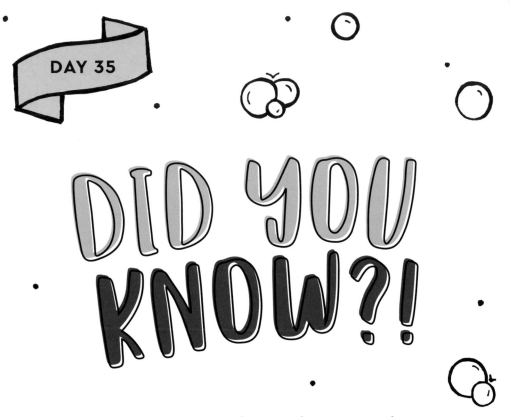

DID YOU KNOW?!

My son [or daughter], be attentive to my words;
incline your ear to my sayings. Let them not escape from
your sight; keep them within your heart. For they are life
to those who find them, and healing to all their flesh.

Proverbs 4:20-22

. . . .

**Did you know that God's Word has the ability to give you
a great life and make you feel better when you are sick?**
All you have to do is basically what you are doing right now.
Read and study God's Word, ask your mom and dad questions if you don't understand what it's saying, and then put
those things into practice.

The more carefully you follow these words, the better your life gets. And though it *doesn't* mean everything will always be awesome and that you'll never get sick, it **does** mean that you have the power of God working on the inside of you—how cool is that?!

What does this mean? What can this power do? Well, God's Word says it can heal you when you're not feeling well. And I've been there before, too! I know what it's like to not feel well. So, sure, I go to the doctor and take medicine, but I've also learned it's important to say this out loud: "The healing power of God is working in me right now!" That's a promise from the Bible, and one you need to hold onto very tightly!

KID PRAYER

God, help me keep Your words right in front of me at all times, and remember it when I'm sick.

PARENT PRAYER

God, I know many things can distract me as a parent. Help me to focus on all You are; I know doing so will infuse my life with Your goodness.

SHARING IS CARING

Do not neglect to do good and to share what you have, for such sacrifices are pleasing to God.

Hebrews 13:16

Today, some of your friends may end up at your house or you'll go to the playground with some kids and their parents. Everyone will be playing, and tasty snacks might also make an appearance. And the minute they do, your mom or dad says, "Make sure you share!" At first, you don't want to share. You don't want to give someone else something that's yours. You want what you want.

But why is sharing so important? God's Word says, "For God so loved the world that He gave His only Son..." Simply, God

shared Jesus with everyone who was and will ever be born on the planet. And Jesus didn't *have* to come, but He *chose* to because of His great love for everyone.

And just like God shared Jesus with you, you should always try to be a good sharer with others. When you do, you are acting a lot like God. And parents feel pretty great when they see their kids doing something good—and God is the very same when He watches you too!

When you don't feel like sharing your toys, snacks or turns at the playground, but you do it anyway, God looks at you and says, "Wow! I'm so proud of you! And, you made your friend pretty happy too!" And keep in mind this truth God taught me a long time ago: *Your attitude belongs to you, and only you can decide what it's going to be.*

KID PRAYER
. . . .

God, help me to share what I have like I am sharing it with You!

PARENT PRAYER
. . . .

God, just like You have been good to me, help me look for those in need who I can be good to!

A BRAND NEW MIND!

**Do not be conformed to this world,
but be transformed by the renewal of your mind,
that by testing you may discern what is the will of God,
what is good and acceptable and perfect.**
Romans 12:2

Are you ready for this? God renews your mind! That's right. He renews it (which means *He makes it fresh every day*). But it's not something that just happens on its own. You have to wake up and ask God to renew your mind—for a fresh start each day!

Your mind is an incredible thing! It stores memories (remember the first time you learned to ride your bike), it helps you figure out math problems (5 + 5 is __), and it helps you understand the difference between right and wrong. But there's a catch! If you are trying to do all of these things without asking God to help you, it can actually do the opposite.

Instead of helping, your thoughts can hurt you. You can remember things you shouldn't (like feelings of guilt). You can spend too much time trying to figure things out instead of trusting God. And instead of being really clear and understanding something, you can feel all cloudy and confused.

God doesn't want any of that for you! He wants you to have a clear mind—one that feels fresh and is ready to face anything! So how do you renew your mind? Read His Word and ask Him for help, and don't do anything that you feel like God doesn't want you to do.

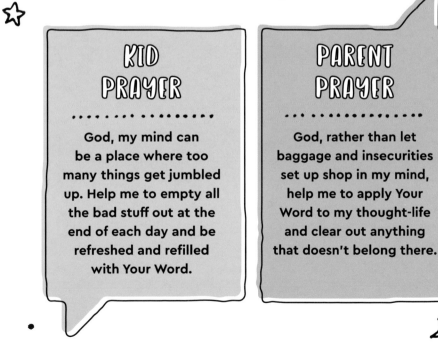

KID PRAYER

God, my mind can be a place where too many things get jumbled up. Help me to empty all the bad stuff out at the end of each day and be refreshed and refilled with Your Word.

PARENT PRAYER

God, rather than let baggage and insecurities set up shop in my mind, help me to apply Your Word to my thought-life and clear out anything that doesn't belong there.

KNOCK KNOCK...

For God gave us a spirit not of fear but of power and love and self-control.
2 Timothy 1:7

Have you ever had to deal with a friend who's not being nice to you? Maybe they are being mean to you at school and doing very unkind things to you. So, what happens when one afternoon you hear a knock at the door and you *know* it's them? You feel fear and worry inside of your stomach. You **really** don't want to answer the door because they've not been nice...so what do you do?

It would be easy to answer the door feeling full of fear. But, it would be **so brave** to answer the door full of confidence and love. You might not even want to do that, so you tell your mom or dad what's going on and **they** answer the door full of confidence and love. Either way, when you think something is going to be scary, ask God to help you trust Him and answer that knocking with faith. After all, fear is **just** a feeling and will eventually go away. God can help you do it afraid!

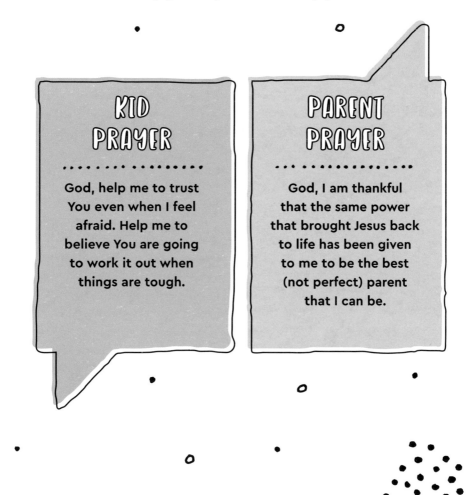

KID PRAYER

God, help me to trust You even when I feel afraid. Help me to believe You are going to work it out when things are tough.

PARENT PRAYER

God, I am thankful that the same power that brought Jesus back to life has been given to me to be the best (not perfect) parent that I can be.

TIME TO BOARD!

**Do not be anxious about anything, but in everything
by prayer and supplication with thanksgiving let your requests
be made known to God. And the peace of God,
which surpasses all understanding, will guard your hearts
and your minds in Christ Jesus.**
Philippians 4:6-7

Have you ever flown on a plane? The first time may have been a little strange—you might have even been a little scared. You get to the airport, and there are a lot of people running around. You move through a machine that you've never seen before and you may even get to stand on a moving walkway.

On the plane, you hear someone say, "prepare for takeoff," and the plane starts racing down the runway. You go faster and faster and after a few seconds, you feel the plane lift off the ground. With a few bumps and dips, the plane starts to climb. You're feeling a little nervous as you look to your parents, hoping this is all very normal.

But after what seems like forever, and you look out the window, you are very surprised by what you see! The bumps and dips stopped, and you see the sun shining and the clouds are puffy and white. It's beautiful!

Notice what happened? Something that was new to you that made you nervous now puts a smile on your face and is not scary at all! You've had a new experience and it's taught you something very valuable: Something may seem scary at first, but sometimes it's really amazing on the other side! God never leaves you or forsakes you—even when things are new or scary. His peace is always there for you!

KID PRAYER

God, I want to be open to new experiences. Help me to jump into the adventure!

PARENT PRAYER

God, when a new challenge comes my way with my kids, I will not worry. Help me to confidently know that You will equip and give me all that I need to respond in the right way.

ROLL CALL

**And let us not grow weary of doing good,
for in due season we will reap, if we do not give up.**
Galatians 6:9

Does your teacher take attendance each morning? They go through a list and they call out each and every name. But have you ever wondered why they do it? In many ways, it's a very simple answer. They call your name to make sure you are **there**.

But here's something I'd like for you to think about for a minute: When they call your name, you are **more** than just that name. You are a great and detailed mixture of gifts, abilities and personality. Simply put, no one on the planet is like you!

So, when they call out your name, you not only respond with "Here!" but you also can respond in the confidence that God made you just as you are. Maybe you are a very kind person, perhaps you are very outgoing. You might be good at sports or you might love science and doing experiments. You might be shy, you might like to sing, or maybe you're super-good at roller-hockey. But whatever it is, when you respond with "Here," you are bringing **everything** of who you are to the world!

You don't have to compare yourself to others and you can be happy for your friends who aren't like you. **Without you**, the world would be missing something pretty awesome. So today, be who God made you to be and confidently embrace it (which means *to hold on and love something that's very special*).

KID PRAYER

God, help me to be me! I'm grateful for all the ways You created me— that You have worked out all the details about me.

PARENT PRAYER

God, I am an "everything nothing"—I am everything in You and nothing outside of You! I have nothing to worry about!

God made this day and

I'm going to enjoy it

HAPPY!

Psalm 118:24

DAY 41

GUESS WHAT HE SAID?

...Our purpose is to please God, not people.
He alone examines the motives of our hearts.
1 Thessalonians 2:4 (NLT)

• •

Today, you'll find yourself sitting in a classroom, at a lunch table or at a park, and you'll have a chance to talk to your friends. You might talk about what you like or don't like about school. Maybe you'll talk about an upcoming vacation or something fun you get to do. But, then the topic may change to something **else**.

Someone might say, "Do you know Liam? He's super-mean and I don't think we should talk to him anymore." And another person might chime in with, "Liam? Yeah, he's not nice, but you should meet his sister Grace! She's even worse!"

And then everyone will look at you. What will **you** say? Will you chime in and talk badly about them or will you respond with something else? You know it's a simple choice—you should do the right thing—but you **really** want to be included!

But at the end of the day, it's more important to be a kind person and stick up for people than to go with the crowd and be mean.

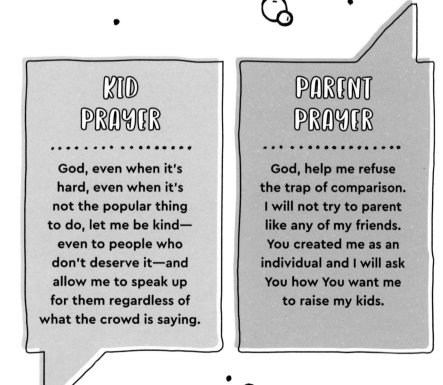

KID PRAYER

God, even when it's hard, even when it's not the popular thing to do, let me be kind—even to people who don't deserve it—and allow me to speak up for them regardless of what the crowd is saying.

PARENT PRAYER

God, help me refuse the trap of comparison. I will not try to parent like any of my friends. You created me as an individual and I will ask You how You want me to raise my kids.

CANDYLAND'S JUST A PLACE TO VISIT

Whatever you do, work heartily, as for the Lord and not for men, knowing that from the Lord you will receive the inheritance as your reward. You are serving the Lord Christ.

Colossians 3:23-24

Who doesn't love a big bag of candy? Maybe you've gotten a big bag of candy for your birthday or a basket of candy at Easter...or maybe your grandma and grandpa just like to stuff you with candy when you go over to their house? I know I like to give some to my grandkids. But even though candy is delicious, you can't live and always eat candy.

If you did, you'd quickly learn how bad it makes you feel. The reason is this: God did not create your body to constantly

eat candy. There is a reason there are little round green things that show up on your plate at dinner. Yes, you may think, *Yuck! Peas! They are disgusting.* But they are the fuel your body needs to give you energy. A land of candy is fun to visit every now and again, but you can't move in!

And just like you can't live on candy alone, God does the very same thing when it comes to helping you grow as a little Christian into a full-grown, adult one. Instead of having fun **all** the time, He teaches you responsibility...instead of changing your clothes and leaving them on the floor, you learn to pick them up and put them in the laundry basket.

So, put a smile on your face when you have to do something that doesn't seem too fun at first. It's likely you are learning a skill that will help you out a lot once you are older!

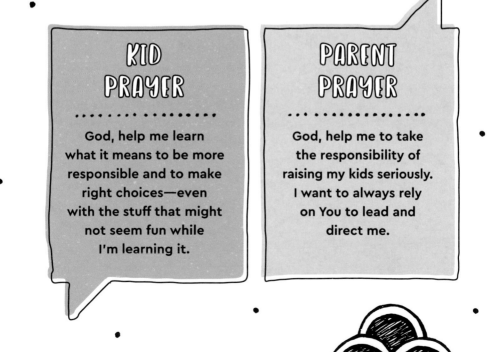

KID PRAYER

God, help me learn what it means to be more responsible and to make right choices—even with the stuff that might not seem fun while I'm learning it.

PARENT PRAYER

God, help me to take the responsibility of raising my kids seriously. I want to always rely on You to lead and direct me.

GOD IS ALL AROUND YOU

**Because he holds fast to me in love, I will deliver him;
I will protect him, because he knows my name. When he calls
to me, I will answer him; I will be with him in trouble;
I will rescue him and honor him.**
Psalm 91:14-15

God is big—like really big. And when you get in trouble, you need to remember that He does not run away from you in those moments. Nope! He is right there. For instance, if there's a situation at school where someone is being a bully and bringing trouble to you, God is there.

Now, here is something really important: God doesn't like it when someone is mean to you, and He wants you to know

that He loves you and likes who you are. In fact, God's Word says that He surrounds you in those moments. Like a big hug from your grandparents, His arms wrap around you. Why? Because you have to remember that God is always with you!

Look up, there is God! Turn to your right and to your left... who is there? It's God. Always. So, although you may have moments where you feel alone, you're not. You have a God who shows up. You have a God who completely and totally surrounds you. And because of it, you can take a deep breath no matter what's going on. You can rest in that *surrounded* kind of love.

KID PRAYER

. . . .

God, help me to see You when things are tricky. When someone has done something wrong to me, help me to know You are with me.

PARENT PRAYER

. . . .

God, I know I'll face tough parenting moments and make mistakes, but help me not to confuse my *who* with my *do*. I know that You surround me and will give me the strength to walk through it!

WHAT'S THE PLAN?

Blessed is the man who walks not in the counsel of the wicked, nor stands in the way of sinners, nor sits in the seat of scoffers; but his delight is in the law of the Lord, and on his law he meditates day and night.

Psalm 1:1-2

Today, you may have a plan that seems pretty clear. You'll go to school, do some spelling, work on math, learn about some of the presidents and then you'll come home. You'll play outside for a little bit, do some homework, have dinner and then get ready for bed. Those are all the things that will happen without giving it much thought.

But as you go through the day, what's happening on the **inside?** What are you *thinking* about? Are you thinking about how God would act during class? Are you wondering what Jesus would do at recess? Or are you just floating through the day not giving too much thought to that stuff? It's important that we have God in mind even in the everyday stuff—that we do our best to act the way God would want us to.

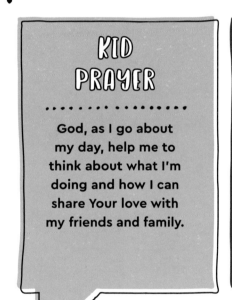

KID PRAYER

God, as I go about my day, help me to think about what I'm doing and how I can share Your love with my friends and family.

PARENT PRAYER

God, I refuse to allow the corruption and negativity of this world to overwhelm me. Help me to make *Your* opinion the only standard in my life.

WANNA KNOW A SECRET?

Study this Book of Instruction continually. Meditate on it day and night so you will be sure to obey everything written in it. Only then will you prosper and succeed in all you do.
Joshua 1:8 (NLT)

When you study God's Word, it's like learning the best secret ever! It has the power to help you be the best you can be, but only if you study it. So, every time you open it up, you should ask God to help you understand what He's saying and then put it into practice.

No matter how old you are or what you are going through, the Bible has the answer to every single question. It's like

God has taken the time to write you a personalized letter with detailed instructions on how to live your life!

Not sure how to deal with a tricky situation with a friend at school? Study God's Word on the topic of walking in love. Angry about not getting the part in the school play? Study scriptures on anger and what to do when you are upset. Feel like you don't belong? Study on the topic of how much God loves you and the amazing plans He has for your life!

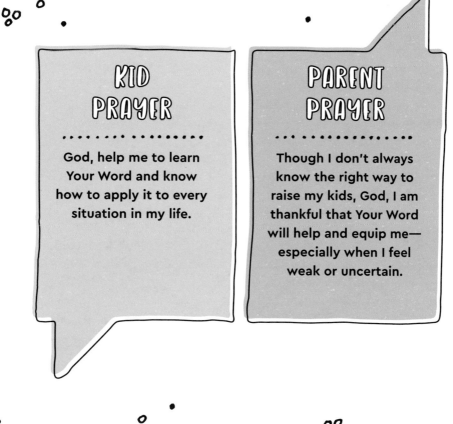

KID PRAYER

God, help me to learn Your Word and know how to apply it to every situation in my life.

PARENT PRAYER

Though I don't always know the right way to raise my kids, God, I am thankful that Your Word will help and equip me—especially when I feel weak or uncertain.

I HAVE DECIDED

Again Jesus spoke to them, saying, "I am the light of the world. Whoever follows me will not walk in darkness, but will have the light of life."
John 8:12

. . . .

You are going to make lots of decisions today. You'll have to choose your clothes. You'll have to decide what you want to eat for lunch and where to sit. You'll have to choose to listen and learn during history, and you'll have to choose to respond the right way when something is going wrong. Basically, you make about a thousand decisions a day, and some are a little silly and some are pretty serious.

But the most important decision you have to make is to choose to follow Jesus! It's not a decision you just make once. And it's not a decision you make just when everything is going right and the sun is shining or when things are hard and it's pouring down rain.

You have to decide to follow and listen to Jesus when everything makes sense and when NOTHING makes sense. You have to be committed (which means *to make up your mind and never change it*) and trust God for it all. It's important to say something like that each and every day. After all, God is bigger and stronger than anything, and He wins every time!

So, wherever you are in your day, take a minute to say out loud, "Jesus, I choose You, and I will follow and obey You no matter what."

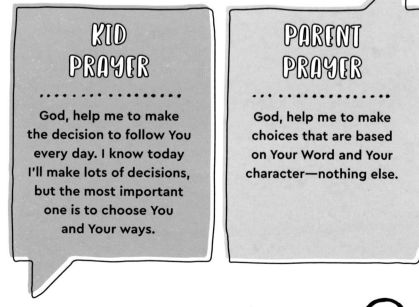

KID PRAYER

· · · · · · · · · · · · · ·

God, help me to make the decision to follow You every day. I know today I'll make lots of decisions, but the most important one is to choose You and Your ways.

PARENT PRAYER

· · · · · · · · · · · · · ·

God, help me to make choices that are based on Your Word and Your character—nothing else.

BOWLING BUMPERS

**In all your ways acknowledge him,
and he will make straight your paths.**
Proverbs 3:6

• • • • • • • • • • • • • • • • • • •

Have you ever gone to a birthday bowling party? Maybe you've gone to a bowling alley when you were younger and needed to use the bumpers. The bumpers are helpful because they keep your bowling ball from rolling into the gutter. And everyone knows the best position to roll the ball is right down the middle!

Being in the gutter is no fun because you don't get any points! And just like bowling, in life you will have to do your best to stay out of the gutters. There are gutters of gossip, gutters of a bad attitude, gutters of negativity and gutters of guilt...but all of them are just a big waste of time!

God has a great plan for your life. One that keeps you right in the middle, heading full steam ahead. And even when you make a mistake or accidentally start to wander toward the gutters, if you trust God and ask Him for help, He will make the bumpers pop right up!

KID PRAYER

. . . .

God, though I always do my best, there will be moments where I start to stray toward the gutters. Help me to realize it quickly and call out to You.

PARENT PRAYER

. . . .

God, help me to guide my kids on the path You've established for them. I will help them navigate it and teach them to be patient in the process.

TAKE A LOOK!

**Draw near to God,
and he will draw near to you....**
James 4:8

Sometimes to hear and understand God, you have to get as close as possible to Him. Just like a magnifying glass or a microscope at school, the closer you look, the more you see. Think about looking at a leaf or rock with a magnifying glass or microscope...you walk by these two objects every day, but when you stop and really give them a good look, so many more details are revealed. You see things you didn't see before. You can see all the different layers that make up the rock, you can see the veins and ways the leaves are made. Though you can't really see them with your regular eyes, the microscope supercharges what you see!

Want to learn more about God? Get as close as possible to Him and ask Him to let you zoom in and see all the details of His character (which means *what makes God, God!*). The closer you look, the more you'll see...and then, when you see God more clearly, you'll have a better idea of who He is and what He would do in any situation. And bam! You become supercharged too!

KID PRAYER

God, show me what You look like up close— I want to see all the details of who You are.

PARENT PRAYER

God, when I have days that I'm tired and worn out, help me to draw close to You and renew my strength.

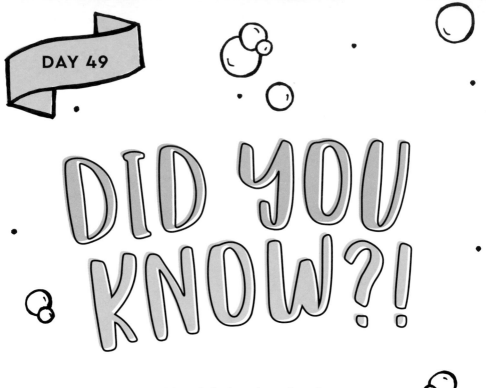

DID YOU KNOW?!

I will walk in freedom, for I have
devoted myself to your commandments.
Psalm 119:45 (NLT)

Did you know God will help you carry the weight of life?
Have you ever had your feelings hurt? Or maybe you made a
wrong choice at school? When you carry the guilt of doing
something you shouldn't have—or the pain of being hurt—it
can make your whole body feel heavy. You can feel like your
backpack is filled with bricks!

But this isn't how God wants you to feel! In both of those moments, He wants you to come to Him. He wants to hear from

you. He wants you to ask Him for help. No matter what's happened or what you've done, God is faithful and will help you.

Here is a great promise from God's Word: When you follow Him, and do your best to follow His Word, it will make you strong, confident (which means *you feel good about what you're doing*), and maybe even feel a little easier.

So, the moment life starts to feel heavy, stop right then and there and go to God. And whether that's through prayer or reading the Bible, be quick to respond and get that weight off your shoulders!

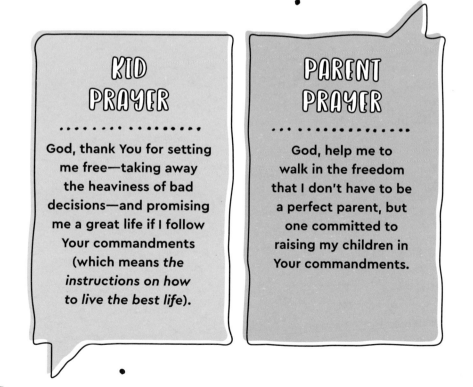

KID PRAYER

. . . .

God, thank You for setting me free—taking away the heaviness of bad decisions—and promising me a great life if I follow Your commandments (which means *the instructions on how to live the best life*).

PARENT PRAYER

. . . .

God, help me to walk in the freedom that I don't have to be a perfect parent, but one committed to raising my children in Your commandments.

CRASHING WAVES

**As for me, I shall behold your face in righteousness;
when I awake, I shall be satisfied with your likeness.**
Psalm 17:15

Have you ever been to the ocean? Maybe it was on a family vacation or a school trip. Can you think about what it looked like? What it smelled like? Did you just stand there staring at how awesome it was? How big it was? How pretty?

Or are you one of those kids who doesn't think but just runs to stuff like that? Were you so excited about being there that you took off as soon as the car stopped? You jumped feet first into where the sand met the ocean waves and squished the goop through your toes?

And though you won't wake up at the beach every day (unless you're lucky enough to live there), or even if you've never been, you do know how awesome it is. You do know the feeling of being excited and wanting to run straight into it! This is the way God wants us to get our day started: full of wonder that He has given us another day and excitement to take on the big, wide spaces He's created!

KID PRAYER

God, today I am going to live in awe and wonder of what You're doing. Help me to be excited about all the things that will come my way and to appreciate them.

PARENT PRAYER

God, help me to understand that my identity as a parent is not in my ability to provide my kids with material things, but to make sure they know how magnificent and life-changing Jesus is!

It doesn't matter who's against me, because

GOD IS ON MY SIDE

Romans 8:31

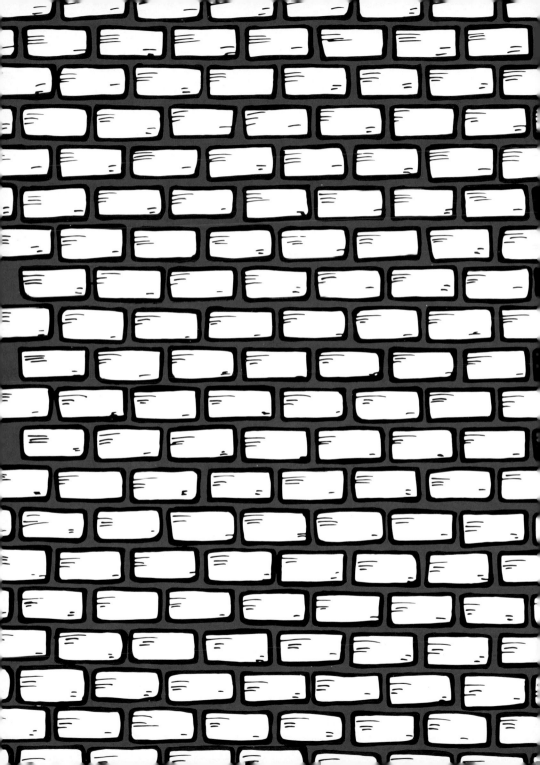

IT'S TIME TO PARTY!

**These things I have spoken to you,
that my joy may be in you, and that your joy may be full.**
John 15:11

. . . .

Here's the deal: God wants you to enjoy your life. He wants to hear you laughing a lot. He wants to see that great smile show up on your face. He wants you to have fun with your family and friends. He wants you to be so grateful for His son, Jesus, that you do your best to tell others about Him. He wants you to have a great, over-the-top awesome, filled-with-His-presence kind of life!

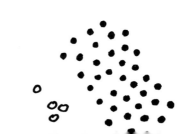

So, sometimes, you just have to slow down and choose to have a mini-party. Yep! That's right! You don't have to always race off to the next thing. If you had a good day at school, celebrate it. Take some time that night to be happy and thank God for helping you have that good day. If you passed a big test, maybe you and your parents can celebrate with some ice cream.

A party doesn't need to be this elaborate (which means *lots and lots of details*) thing. It's a moment to stop and say, "God, because You are with me, I did really well today and I'm going to celebrate it!"

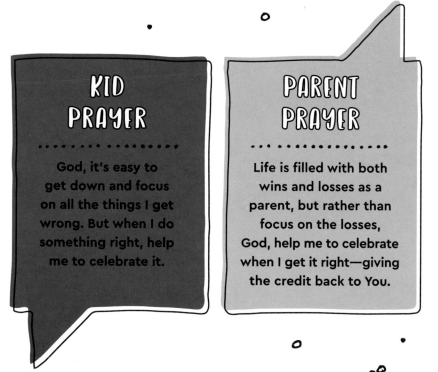

KID PRAYER

God, it's easy to get down and focus on all the things I get wrong. But when I do something right, help me to celebrate it.

PARENT PRAYER

Life is filled with both wins and losses as a parent, but rather than focus on the losses, God, help me to celebrate when I get it right—giving the credit back to You.

IF YOU'RE GONNA DREAM, MAKE SURE IT'S MASSIVE!

And it shall come to pass afterward, that I will
pour out my Spirit on all flesh; your sons and your daughters
shall prophesy, your old men shall dream dreams,
and your young men shall see visions.

Joel 2:28

. . . .

What kind of dreams do you have for your life? Are you dreaming that one day you'll be a singer? Play sports in the major leagues? Do you dream about being an artist, a doctor, or maybe someone who works with kids? When you close your eyes (at night or even in the middle of the day), what do you see?

Here's the deal though: If you're gonna dream, dream big-ol', God-inspired dreams. It's clear when you read God's Word that He has awesome things planned for you. He wants you to have a great life. He wants you to love your life, and He wants you to help others along the way.

It's easy to think small. It's easy to think you shouldn't dream big dreams, especially if you've had a tough life, but don't give in to that! You have greatness inside of you. You have God on your side, and as long as He says you can have it, you need to go after it! Remember, it's better to have a crazy-huge dream and get most of it than dream a teeny-tiny dream and get all of it!

I've said it before, and right now, I want you to read it and then say it out loud: "I expect something good is going to happen to me and through me today!"

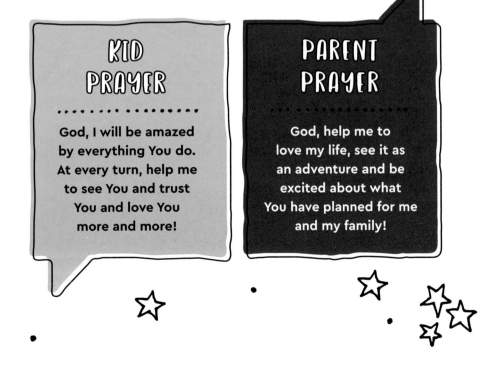

KID PRAYER

God, I will be amazed by everything You do. At every turn, help me to see You and trust You and love You more and more!

PARENT PRAYER

God, help me to love my life, see it as an adventure and be excited about what You have planned for me and my family!

GOD'S WORD = MORE PEACE

**Great peace have those who love your law;
nothing can make them stumble.**
Psalm 119:165

Peace is the amazing, calm feeling we have inside, even when things aren't perfect. But peace doesn't come with having more stuff, and it doesn't come from everyone liking you. Peace comes when you spend lots and lots of time with God. For example, you've been doing these devotions every day, you've been praying, spending time with your mom or dad, and hopefully you feel very peaceful when you do it!

Peace also keeps you calm when you have a big test coming up or a friend is mad at you. It doesn't change the situation, but it changes you. Rather than being upset and worried, you are calm, cool and collected.

And the more you love God and His Word, the more peace you will have. Think about it like this: Have you ever gotten warm clothes right out of the dryer and buried yourself underneath them? If you haven't, ask your parents to do it for you. And when you are sitting underneath the warmth of a heavy blanket, think to yourself, *This is how God's peace feels!*

It surrounds you. It makes you feel safe. So, get as close to God as you can! The more God, the more peace!

KID PRAYER

God, surround
me with Your peace!
Let me sit under
the warmth of
Your love.

PARENT PRAYER

God, help me to
hold on to Your Word.
Even when I'm anxious
about my kids, let me
walk in Your peace
and hold fast to
Your grace.

HOW ABOUT THEM APPLES?

But the Holy Spirit produces this kind of fruit in our lives: love, joy, peace, patience, kindness, goodness, faithfulness, gentleness, and self-control....
Galatians 5:22-23 (NLT)

· ·

Have you ever gone apple picking? Perhaps you've gone on a school field trip where you set off on the bus on a cool fall morning and you and your friends raced down the orchard to snag a few tasty apples! But let me ask you a very silly question: What makes an apple orchard an apple orchard and not a park? Or a field? Think about it—it will only take you a second I'm sure!

Did you guess *apples*...or maybe *fruit?* If you did, you're right! The thing that makes an apple orchard an apple orchard is...**fruit!**

And as Christians, we also produce fruit—just not like the kind you eat. God has given us the ability to produce the fruit of the Spirit (which means *the things God has given us to use while we live on earth*). It's the fruit of love, joy, peace, patience, kindness, goodness, faithfulness, gentleness and self-control! Phew! That's one long list!

And here's the best thing about fruit: Fruit just *is*. You can tell what an apple is just by looking at it. Apples don't have to scream from the branch: "I'm an apple! Seriously guys, look at me! You're looking at an apple!"

So, think about how you can "show" some of the fruit God is helping you produce today!

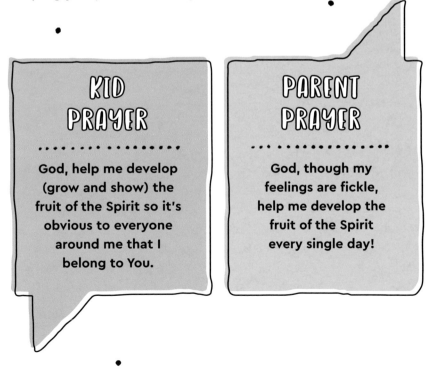

KID PRAYER
. . . .
God, help me develop (grow and show) the fruit of the Spirit so it's obvious to everyone around me that I belong to You.

PARENT PRAYER
. . . .
God, though my feelings are fickle, help me develop the fruit of the Spirit every single day!

DAY 55

BUT...I'M...NOT... SLEEP... ZZZZZZZ

**Dear friend, I pray that you may enjoy
good health and that all may go well with you,
even as your soul is getting along well.**
3 John 1:2 (NIV)

• • • • • • • • • • • • • • • • • • • •

There's not a kid on the planet who wants to hear these words: *It's time for bed!* You've had a great day hanging out with your friends—maybe you went to dinner with another family. Now you're home, getting ready for bed, but you don't want to go to sleep yet! You want to stay up and have fun—play with your siblings or slobbery dog!

Well, you may not want to hear this, but sleep is so good for you! It's not just something your parents tell you. It's

true! God made our bodies to need R.E.S.T. In fact, even God rested on the seventh day of creation! Think about that! He wanted you to see that rest is super-duper important. And you may think, *Resting is boring!* But if you want to be ready for your day tomorrow, you have to rest well today. Especially if you have a big test or the championship game. Resting gives you all the strength you'll need!

And without it, it's going to be pretty tough! When you rest, your body gets a break and goes to work fixing things and filling up your energy levels. So, yes, you may be sleeping, but your body isn't! It's getting you ready for the next day. And there are so many great things that will happen tomorrow and you'll want to be ready to go!

KID PRAYER

God, help me get the rest I need to be as healthy as possible!

PARENT PRAYER

God, help me to take good care of myself. Help me to make good decisions now so I can be healthy for my kids and help them as they grow.

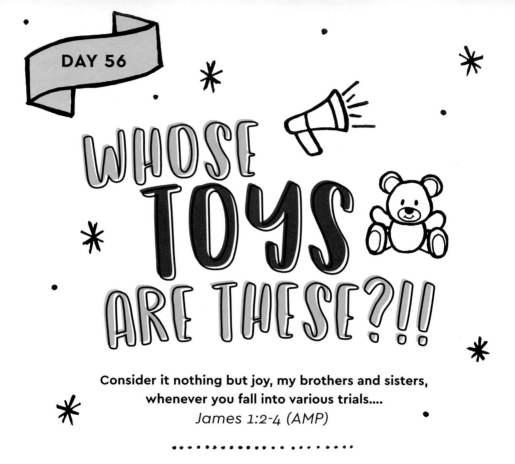

DAY 56

WHOSE TOYS ARE THESE?!!

Consider it nothing but joy, my brothers and sisters, whenever you fall into various trials....
James 1:2-4 (AMP)

• •

Does that phrase sound familiar? Maybe you're sitting in your room one day reading a book and you hear your parents loudly say (*they scream so loud that you think they have a megaphone*) "Whose toys are these!?" In that moment, you have a choice—you fess up and admit that you didn't pick up after yourself. Or, you pretend you don't hear anything and ignore them.

But the question comes again, and instead of a loud voice, the megaphone has become more like a big speaker at a concert: "Whose toys are these??!!" Yep. Now you can hear it. The silence hasn't had any effect on them—they still want someone to answer.

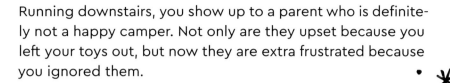

Running downstairs, you show up to a parent who is definitely not a happy camper. Not only are they upset because you left your toys out, but now they are extra frustrated because you ignored them.

As you are cleaning up, your mom or dad asks, "Why don't you just clean them up when you are done with them?" This is a good question to ask yourself. Why didn't you just clean up after yourself? Why not just put the toys away without being asked and avoid (which means *you wouldn't have to even deal with it*) all the extra hassle it caused?

I say it like this: *Take time to deal with little problems and you won't have to spend more time dealing with big ones.* Every moment can teach you something if you are looking for the lesson. Always look for the lesson. God will help you see and learn it if you ask Him for help.

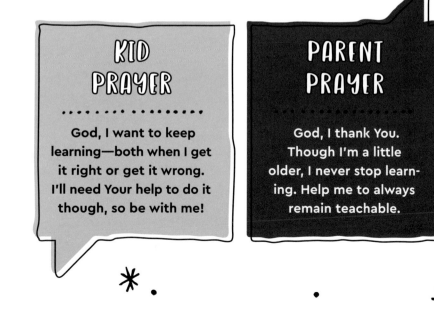

KID PRAYER

God, I want to keep learning—both when I get it right or get it wrong. I'll need Your help to do it though, so be with me!

PARENT PRAYER

God, I thank You. Though I'm a little older, I never stop learning. Help me to always remain teachable.

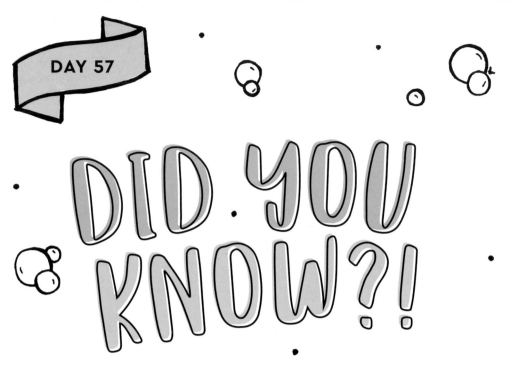

DID YOU KNOW?!

In the beginning, God created the heavens and the earth. The earth was without form and void, and darkness was over the face of the deep. And the Spirit of God was hovering over the face of the waters.

And God said....
Genesis 1:1-3

· ·

Did you know that God created everything around you with His words? That's right. God spoke it and it became something. He thought about a massive mountain, opened His mouth to call it a "mountain" and bam—a mountain appeared. He looked around and thought, *You know, snow on top of that mountain would look great, and bam!* He said "snow," and snow appeared. He wondered what it would look like if the snow was carried down on currents of air, and out of His mouth He whispered, "wind," and the snow swirled around, creating the most incredible patterns of "falling snow."

You see, God speaks, and things happen. And God has given you the very same ability! It doesn't mean you speak and get everything you want. But you *can* speak and pray for all the things God's Word says you can have (which is a LOT, because He only wants the best for you!).

It's important to speak good things—God things—because your words are very important. They have the ability to change both your circumstances *and* your attitude.

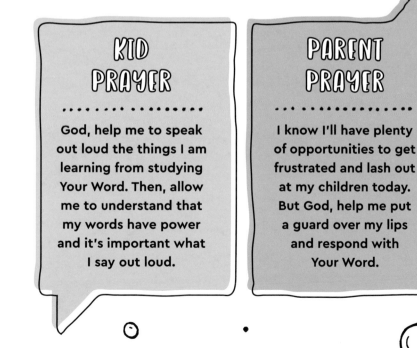

KID PRAYER

. . . .

God, help me to speak out loud the things I am learning from studying Your Word. Then, allow me to understand that my words have power and it's important what I say out loud.

PARENT PRAYER

. . . .

I know I'll have plenty of opportunities to get frustrated and lash out at my children today. But God, help me put a guard over my lips and respond with Your Word.

THE BEST GIFT. EVER.

Thank God! Call out his Name!
Tell the whole world who he is and what he's done!...
1 Chronicles 16:8 (MSG)

What's one of the best things about a big, wrapped gift? Maybe one you get on your birthday or for Christmas? Is it the wrapping? The big bow? Nope! It's what's hiding underneath—what's inside the box. And when you finally get permission to tear into it, what happens?

There are probably lots of screams of joy, giggles, laughter—you can't get to the gift fast enough. And once you do—once you finally see what it is—you scream out to everyone in the room, "It's the exact thing I wanted! Thanks Mom and Dad!"

Jesus came to earth as a gift to **all** of us. All we have to do is open it up and see the great life He has for us. And just like any good gift, the best part is not just getting it, but being thankful about it and telling everyone how amazing it is! Who can you think about who would love a gift like that? What person in your life needs the gift of Jesus?

KID PRAYER

Thanks, God, for the gift of You! You sure are good and I'm about to run out of here and tell everyone about You.

PARENT PRAYER

I'm grateful today, God, that You've given me the privilege and responsibility of caring for my kids and teaching them about Your Word. Help me to stay thankful!

MEANIE PANTS

Get rid of all bitterness, rage and anger, brawling and slander, along with every form of malice.
Ephesians 4:31 (NIV)

Does this sound familiar? You head to the lunchroom and your friends are at a table in the corner, laughing and talking. When you sit down at the table, you realize they are making fun of another kid in class. They are making fun of the way he dresses—saying his clothes look terrible and dirty. They are also laughing and talking loudly about the way he talks. When he gets nervous in front of his class, he stutters and has a hard time sharing with the class.

You know right away what they are doing is wrong. You know you should say something. So, the question is, "What do you do?" Do you stop the conversation and tell your friends that's not how to treat anyone? Or do you join in and make fun of him as well?

But you don't want your friends to get mad at you or make fun of *you*...and most importantly, you don't want them to exclude you (which means *to leave you out*).

Here's a quick secret: If they are going to be mean and make fun of people, it's not worth being around them! In my life, I've found it's very important to keep this thought in mind: *I always care more about what God thinks of me than what other people think of me.*

Instead of putting others down, we can be like Jesus and choose to say good things about people! And when some-one is getting teased (when other kids are being "meanie pants"), we can be their buddy and stick up for them.

KID PRAYER

· · · · · · · · · · · · · · · · ·

God, help me to recognize right and wrong. And once I see it, help me to have the courage to always choose right.

PARENT PRAYER

· · · · · · · · · · · · · · · · ·

It's never okay to repay anger for anger or respond unkindly. God, allow me to understand that my kids are watching, and if I want them to treat others nicely, they have to see me do the same.

ONLY JESUS IS PERFECT!

I considered my ways; I turned my feet to [obey] Your testimonies.
Psalm 119:59 (AMPC)

Besides Jesus, no one has ever lived a perfect life. Not you, not your mom or dad or even your best friend. Everyone makes mistakes. But here's the great news about God's Word. When you study it, you learn right from wrong. It helps you talk in a way that sounds more and more like Jesus. When you are faced with a difficult situation, you can answer like God would!

Though you miss the mark every now and again, God is so good that He gives you the opportunity to have a do-over. When you get mad and blurt out (which means *you say something without thinking first*) mean, ugly words, you should be quick to apologize. And don't worry, God will always help you do it! When you've told a lie about what happened at school or at a friend's house and are caught in that lie, you can ask for forgiveness (from both God and your parents) and then simply move on—guilt-free.

Living with a constant feeling of guilt is not from God. Sure, He wants you to do your best, and admit when you get it wrong, but He does NOT want you to live and walk around like you are a constant mess-up. You're not. Not to God, and not to those around you. They love you so very much!

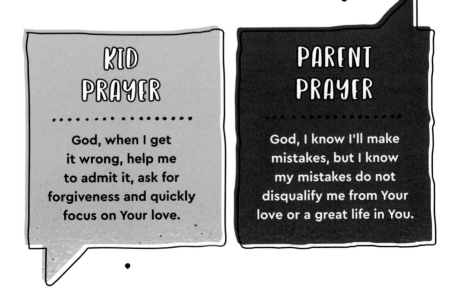

KID PRAYER

God, when I get it wrong, help me to admit it, ask for forgiveness and quickly focus on Your love.

PARENT PRAYER

God, I know I'll make mistakes, but I know my mistakes do not disqualify me from Your love or a great life in You.

GOOD STUFF

out loud—on the outside.

Proverbs 18:21

½ A CUP OF THIS + A TABLESPOON OF THAT

Commit your work to the Lord, and your plans will be established. The Lord has made everything for its purpose, even the wicked for the day of trouble.
Proverbs 16:3-4

· ·

Have you ever made a cake or brownies or cupcakes or anything else that's really delicious? And when you run into the kitchen and they are freshly made and ready to eat, you take a bite or pop one in your mouth and think, *This is the BEST. DESSERT. EVER.*

But did you know that the dessert didn't just poof into existence? Your mom or dad, grandma or grandpa had to make them from a bunch of different ingredients. Flour, chocolate, sugar, brown sugar, baking powder...these are the basic ingredients that make a cake or brownies.

Though the final product is this very yummy thing to eat, the ingredients themselves are not tasty at all (well...maybe the *sugar* is). But if you got out a small spoon and tried to eat the flour or the baking powder by itself, you'd immediately spit it out!

And here's the point: Your life is like one big recipe! You're taking one half cup of confidence and a teaspoon of patience (or maybe a gallon of it) and mixing in a challenging quiz at school or a situation at home that makes you sad. Sure, no one wants the quiz or sadness, but when God is the main ingredient, He can take even these things and make something great out of them. So, when different situations come your way and you don't understand what's going on, just trust that every experience has a place in your life and that ultimately (which means *when things are all done*), you'll turn out to be one fantastic kid!

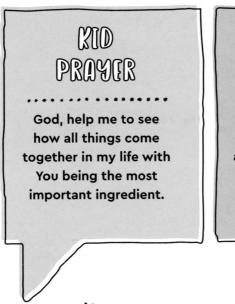

KID PRAYER

. . . .

God, help me to see how all things come together in my life with You being the most important ingredient.

PARENT PRAYER

. . . .

God, help me to understand what You are calling my kids to do and I will do my best to add value to the various ingredients needed.

PRACTICE MAKES PERFECT

I can do all things through him who strengthens me.
Philippians 4:13

Do you know what that phrase means? It means if you want to get good at something—**anything**—you need to practice! And how you practice will determine how well you play.

This might sound a little funny, but when you practice, you are teaching your body to get stronger in the areas you'll need come game time or performance time. You might think, *I'm already strong! That's why I'm playing or participating!* But do you think you are as strong as possible?

When you teach your body to correctly kick a ball, because it's a new skill, you have to do it over and over again to get it right. Obviously, you can't just stop a game in the middle of everything and ask, "Can I do that again?" You practice and prepare ahead of time so you can be ready to go when the game starts!

The same is true with your relationship with Jesus. And although you'll never be perfect at it, you should try your very best to practice and learn as much as possible about how the Bible says you should live your life and treat people. In fact, right now, reading these devotions is doing just that! They are teaching you something about life now so that when you experience something like it, you'll know exactly what to do!

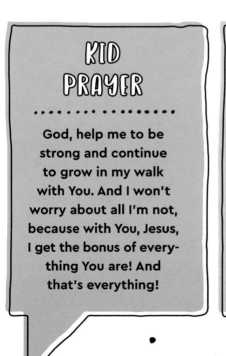

KID PRAYER

God, help me to be strong and continue to grow in my walk with You. And I won't worry about all I'm not, because with You, Jesus, I get the bonus of everything You are! And that's everything!

PARENT PRAYER

No matter what I face today, God, I ask You to be by my side. In You, I can do anything because of the strength You give me.

DID YOU KNOW?!

**Teach me good judgment and knowledge,
for I believe in your commandments.**
Psalm 119:66

· ·

Did you know that when you know God's Word, you know way more than you think? That sounds a little confusing doesn't it? Here's what it means: God's Word is so amazing that it helps you know stuff at your core (which means *deep down you know without knowing*).

Here's an example. Let's say your friends are talking bad about another person and as you are standing there you think, *This doesn't seem right—I don't think I should talk*

bad about another person. Hmmmm! But how did you know that? You know that because you have become a student of God's Word. You are reading it and it's changing you from the inside out.

This is the beauty of God's Word. The more you study it, the more you know it—and not just in one area or another, but in any area you need help! God's Word is like a key to a door that's locked. Sure, you may not immediately know what to do (which key on your keychain opens which door), but over time, you will! You just have to stay committed and never give up!

KID PRAYER

God, when I stop and think really hard, I can only do so much... but when I ask You to give me wisdom, You help me and teach me all I need to know.

PARENT PRAYER

God, help me to be completely dependent on Your Word concerning how I raise my kids. I won't follow trends or how others do it— but solely You!

CAN YOU SEE RESPECT WITH YOUR EYES?

Show proper respect to everyone, love the family of believers, fear God, honor the emperor.
1 Peter 2:17 (NIV)

What does it mean to respect something or someone? What does respect look like? Is it something you can see with your eyes when you're walking down the street? Or do you have to bring life to respect?

Bringing life (which means *putting good action to good thoughts*) to respect is pretty simple. It's making sure you say "thank you" when someone does something for you. It's holding a door open for others, so they can get in and

out before you do. Respect is holding your tongue (which means *to simply say nothing*) when your parents ask you to do something, or opening your mouth when you're in a situation where you need to speak up for a person who is being treated unfairly.

Respect is also something you give to God. When you wake up and tell God how much you need Him, that's respecting Him. Why? Because it's saying "God, You are the most important person in my life and I can't do life without You." Respecting God also happens when you follow His Word! Every time you respond to a situation in the way His Word instructs you to, you are saying, "I know Your words and ways are better than mine."

KID PRAYER
. . . .
God, help me to not only love those around me, but to respect them— even if they see life differently from me.

PARENT PRAYER
. . . .
God, help me to respect my children and teach them that everyone is valuable to You.

EVERY FRECKLE + DIMPLE!

I praise you, for I am fearfully and wonderfully made....
Psalm 139:14

God was very intentional (which means *He took a lot of time to make you just right*) when it came to who you are and all the different things that make you *you!* Every freckle. Every dimple. That teeny tiny birthmark behind your knee—yep! Even that! But what about when someone makes you laugh really hard and you snort? Did God create that too? Guess what? He did!

And He even was very specific to give you the personality you have. Do you not like all your food to touch on your dinner plate? Do you love to read the directions when it comes to a project? Are you more drawn to art over math? Are you comfortable when there are lots of people around, or do you prefer to hang out at home with just a couple friends?

Spoiler alert! **All** of these things have been crafted into who you are. So, you don't have to feel bad or even worry that people won't like who you are. God loves who you are, and He wants **you** to love who you are, too! When you do that, when you don't spend time wishing you were someone else, it sure does make God smile!

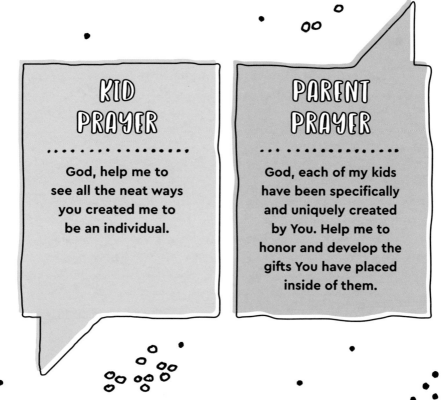

KID PRAYER

God, help me to see all the neat ways you created me to be an individual.

PARENT PRAYER

God, each of my kids have been specifically and uniquely created by You. Help me to honor and develop the gifts You have placed inside of them.

I'VE GOT YOUR BACK

Because of the Lord's great love we are not consumed, for his compassions never fail.
Lamentations 3:22 (NIV)

Do you have a best friend? Someone you play with every day? Maybe it's a neighbor or a cousin who lives close to you. It might even be your brother or sister. And because you play with them so much, you would do anything to help them.

There's a saying you may not have heard before: *I've got your back.* And what that means is that no matter what happens, you will be there for them. It doesn't mean you won't ever have a disagreement with your friend, but that at the end of each day, you believe the best about them and *"have their backs."*

And here's one of the best promises of the Bible: You've got another *Best Friend* out there who will always "have your back." Jesus is that friend. He helps you when you have questions. When you feel uncertain about yourself, He is there to cheer you on and tell you that you can do it! If you feel afraid, He stands next to you to make all the scary stuff run away. And at the start of each day, it's like He's waiting outside to play—He is so excited to spend time with you and help you—and because of it, you are **never alone**.

KID PRAYER

. . . .

God, help me to appreciate (another word for value and respect) Your love. You are there for me each day, so help me to know that if I need a redo, You are happy to give me one.

PARENT PRAYER

. . . .

God, I am never alone. Even when it feels like I've let my kids down, I know that Your grace and mercy strengthens me and fills in any of my gaps, or shortcomings, every day.

HUH?

**It is the glory of God to conceal things,
but the glory of kings is to search things out.**
Proverbs 25:2

. . . .

You might find yourself in a new situation today. It could be in class. It could be with friends learning a new game. Perhaps it's with your team and everyone is trying out a new skill. No matter what the situation is, don't be afraid to ask questions!

Questions are a beautiful thing! Think of them like pieces to a puzzle. At first, you may only see a tiny little corner piece, but the more you work on the puzzle, the more clarity (which is another word for *things being very clear*) you have. The more pieces you put together, the easier it is to see the bigger picture—the one on the outside of the box!

Struggling with a math problem in class? Ask your teacher to help you—ask them a question. You may be surprised that when your teacher takes the time to walk you through the problem, you understand all the steps and it clears up your question!

But if you never ask the question, you'll certainly never get an answer! There also might be times where you ask a question—perhaps to God, Himself, about a situation—and you don't feel like there's an immediate (which means *right away*) answer. But you can know that an answer is on the way! That's another great promise from God! And while He is working on getting that answer to you, He will stick close to your side and help you until it shows up!

KID PRAYER

. . . .

God, help me to ask the questions that help me understand Your thoughts and that draw me closer to You.

PARENT PRAYER

. . . .

God, when I don't understand something, help me to ask good questions. Raising kids is not easy but I know that for every question I have, You are faithful to help me discover the answer.

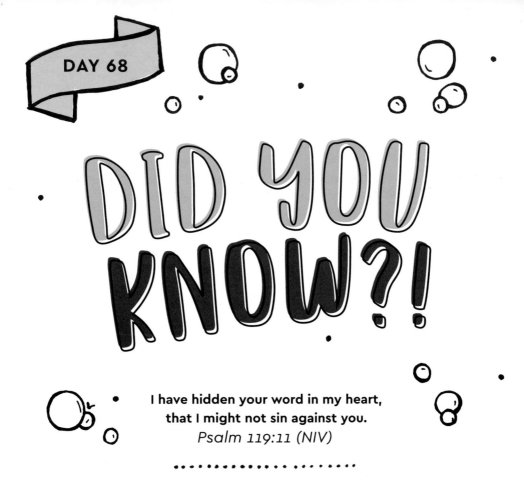

DID YOU KNOW?!

I have hidden your word in my heart,
that I might not sin against you.
Psalm 119:11 (NIV)

Did you know that having *more* of God means having *less* sin in your life? Yep! In some ways it's actually pretty simple. If you see your life as a glass of water, the more water you have inside of that glass means there's less room for anything else.

Now, use that example to think about your own life. The fact is, everyone sins (which means *to not do the thing you know*

God would do). You do. Your mom and dad do. But studying God's Word, having it working inside of your heart and head, fills up your glass. When you don't study God's Word, there is simply nothing in your glass; there is no presence of God's Word, so you will make mistakes and sin more often.

So, don't leave any room in your cup—always make sure God's Word has filled you up!

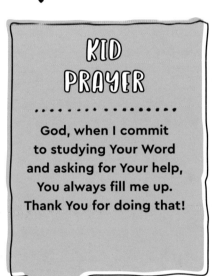

KID PRAYER

God, when I commit to studying Your Word and asking for Your help, You always fill me up. Thank You for doing that!

PARENT PRAYER

God, the only way I will be a successful parent is to fill myself up with Your Word. Help me to not just read it—but study it!

I THINK I'M RIGHT... BUT...

Trust in the Lord with all of your heart, and do not lean on your own understanding. In all your ways acknowledge him, and he will make straight your paths. Be not wise in your own eyes....

Proverbs 3:5-7

Let's learn a **very** important saying. Would you like to know what that saying is? Would you? Okay. Get Ready...here it is...**I think I'm right, but I could be wrong**.

Phew! **There!** Even saying it can make you feel better. And **why** do you feel better about saying it? Because it reminds you that you don't have all the answers. It reminds you that you're not supposed to have all the answers!

And this is how that saying can help you: First, no one is always right. Even if you love being right, it doesn't mean you always will be. In fact, that attitude can cause problems too because being a "know-it-all" makes people feel small and not important. But here's the problem with all of it...

Do you want people to see how smart you are? How you are always right? Or do you want people to see that you rely on God for everything—whether you are right or wrong? If you always want people to say how smart you are, it puts more attention on you and your abilities rather than God, Who **absolutely does** know everything and gives you every bit of wisdom you have.

The reason it's important to learn this and say it out loud is because it shows people around you that you don't always have to be right. That you rely on the God of all truth for every single thing you **do** know!

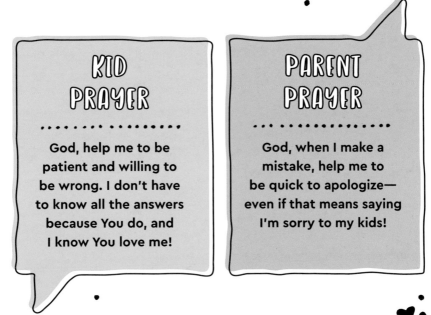

KID PRAYER

God, help me to be patient and willing to be wrong. I don't have to know all the answers because You do, and I know You love me!

PARENT PRAYER

God, when I make a mistake, help me to be quick to apologize— even if that means saying I'm sorry to my kids!

STRONG IN THE STORM

**The name of the Lord is a strong tower;
the righteous man runs into it and is safe.**
Proverbs 18:10

The next time a rain storm rolls through where you live, watch what happens to the trees. The winds kick up and they bend and sway. As you watch the massive trees dance, you start to get concerned and think, *These trees are going to snap and fall over!*

Time goes by, and as the storm passes, the trees are still standing. You think, *How is this possible?* The trees were bending like crazy...they should have been knocked down!

But what keeps them standing? Well, if you had super-powers, your X-ray vision would help you see into the ground and notice tons of roots reaching wider than the tree is tall. And these roots work like a super-strong anchor that holds the tree in place and defends it against the storms.

The Bible tells us it's kind of the same way in our lives, too. You are to be "rooted in God." And just like a tree, when you spend time with God and learn more about Him, every time you pray or trust Him during a storm (*hard times in life are sometimes called storms*), it's making your roots go deeper and wider. So, no matter what comes your way, even if the winds are howling, you may bend and sway some, but you will not break and you will not fall over!

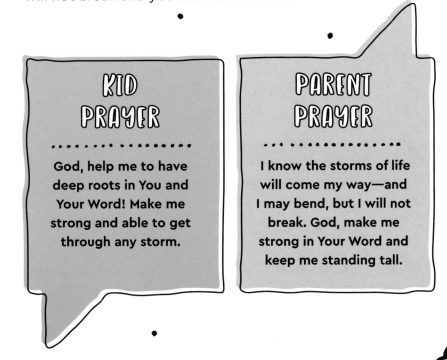

KID PRAYER

God, help me to have deep roots in You and Your Word! Make me strong and able to get through any storm.

PARENT PRAYER

I know the storms of life will come my way—and I may bend, but I will not break. God, make me strong in Your Word and keep me standing tall.

FOR MY GOOD!

Romans 8:28

IN A WORLD FULL OF...

**For we are his workmanship, created in Christ Jesus
for good works, which God prepared beforehand,
that we should walk in them.**

Ephesians 2:10

In a world full of spoons, be a fork. What I mean is...be someone who points others to Jesus even if you are doing it alone. God created you to be a one-of-a-kind person, so you don't have to be like everyone else! At school, be the person who encourages your friends. When people are down, find ways to cheer them up!

You are unique. The people around you are unique and it's all a part of God's plan. You are here to make things better—that's the beauty of it! While people talk about how terrible things are, remind them that there's always something good to find in every situation—even if you have to search for it. When people say, "No way! Not going to happen," you can boldly say, "It doesn't matter how it looks, God always comes through and with Him all things are possible."

The fact is this: You are meant to stand out and bring light, joy and life to the world around you. It's pretty clear that you come across many people who are sad or mad or lonely or grumpy. What better way to brighten their day than to bring fun and laughter to their life? I say it like this: *Our lives are meant to be salty. They should make others thirsty for God.*

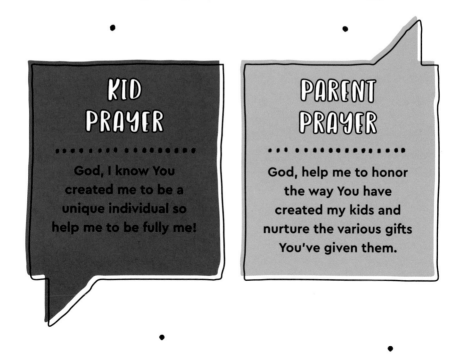

KID PRAYER

God, I know You created me to be a unique individual so help me to be fully me!

PARENT PRAYER

God, help me to honor the way You have created my kids and nurture the various gifts You've given them.

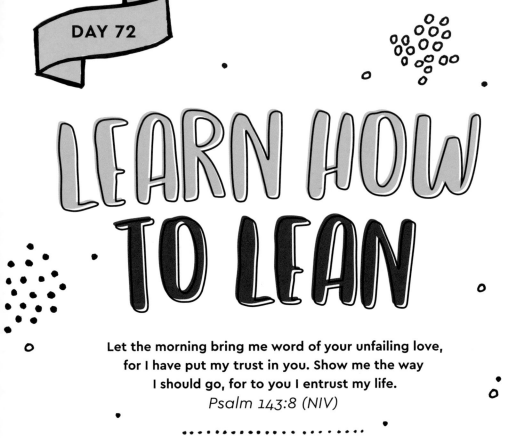

LEARN HOW TO LEAN

**Let the morning bring me word of your unfailing love,
for I have put my trust in you. Show me the way
I should go, for to you I entrust my life.**
Psalm 143:8 (NIV)

After a long day and night of having fun, you might still have some sleepies in your eyes when you make it out to the bus stop. Because the bus comes **so** early! We all have mornings like that. And if you're still a little groggy, you might end up leaning on your mom or dad as you wait for the bus. You know **how** to stand—you do it all the time! But because you're **tired**, it's easier to lean and rely on your mom or dad to prop you up. They help you wait. You lean on them because you know they love you.

Just like leaning on your parents, when you lean on God, you are trusting that He will hold you up. Sure, you can't see God with your regular eyes, but leaning on Him could be as simple as saying, "I've studied for my test and I know God will help me remember the answers." It may even be something like trusting God with a really tough situation. You don't have all the answers, but leaning on Him says, "God, You have all the answers—**help me**."

KID PRAYER

. . . .

God, I know that if I'm tired or scared, You are there to hold me up. Help me to lean on You and trust You in everything I do today.

PARENT PRAYER

. . . .

God, when I feel weak and when I am uncertain about how to raise my kids, help me to cast my cares on You and rely on Your strength.

DID YOU KNOW?!

And the Word became flesh and dwelt among us,
and we have seen his glory, glory as of the
only Son from the Father, full of grace and truth.

John 1:14

Did you know that Jesus *is* the Word of God? Even though that sounds a little confusing, when Jesus came to earth, He brought all of God's (His Dad's) words with Him. Sure, at first, He was a baby—just like you were—but eventually, when He learned to talk, His words were God's words. And since Jesus was born just like you were, you can follow His example.

The more you learn about God, the more you understand how He talks. And you should do your best to talk and act like God. And here's the good news: God will always help you do it! Once you have God's Word inside of you, you'll start to notice how much easier it is to talk and act like Him.

The reason? God's words are incredible! Think about it...the same words that Jesus used in the Bible are the ones you can use and live by, too! And once you start to incorporate (which means *to make them a part of your day and how you speak*) His words, you'll have more energy to take on your day, you won't feel as crabby and you'll see life in a positive way! Life can get tough, but God is tougher! There's nothing you'll go through where God's Word won't show you the way!

KID PRAYER

. . . .

God, help me to learn the importance of Your Word, and help me to use it in every area of my life.

PARENT PRAYER

. . . .

God, there is a lot I don't know, and plenty of moments where I feel ill-equipped for life. But one thing I do know without question is that You love me, and Your Word will always equip me!

GOD LOVES YOU

But God shows his love for us in that while we were still sinners, Christ died for us.
Romans 5:8

Right now, God loves you so very much. And guess what? Yesterday His love for you was just as strong, and tomorrow it will be strong, too! And He doesn't just love you because you always act right or do the right thing. Nope! He knows you will make mistakes and He still loves you!

God's love for you is unconditional (which means *it never ever changes, no matter what*). You didn't have to do anything to make God love you, and there's nothing you can do to make

Him love you less. When you are at your very best, God loves you. When you are at your worst, He loves you still!

And even if you have days where you don't like who you are—maybe you made a big mistake or did something really mean—God still loves you. But how is this possible? God shouldn't like bad behavior or meanness, right? That's true! But I like to say, your "who" is not your "do" (which means that **who** *you are is different from what you* **do**).

Everyone makes mistakes. In fact, if God's love was based on how people acted, everyone would be in big trouble! But thank God, that's not the deal—that's not how God is. He is loving and patient and willing to love us even when we are unlovely. So, you can be confident in God's love for you!

KID PRAYER

. . . .

God, thank you for loving me just as I am—flaws and all!

PARENT PRAYER

. . . .

At both my best and worst, I know you love me, God. Thank You for never wavering or giving up on me.

HE NEVER FAILS

Give thanks to the Lord, for he is good, for his steadfast love endures forever. Give thanks to the God of gods, for his steadfast love endures forever. Give thanks to the Lord of lords, for his steadfast love endures forever.
Psalm 136:1-3

• • • • • • • • • • • • • • • • • • • •

Have you experienced something tough lately? Your feelings were hurt by a friend, you didn't get picked at recess for the team you wanted, or you made a mistake and hurt someone's feelings? Perhaps your best friend moved away, and you are really sad about it...

Here's something to remember: It's okay to be sad. It's okay to feel sadness. But there's also something else to remember:

God loves you, and He is right there with you. He is not scared of sadness and totally understands how you feel.

There's also a chance that you are the one who made a mistake...you said something unkind to hurt someone's feelings. Maybe you lied to your parents about something and you were caught in that lie. Well, guess what? God loves you, and He is right there with you. He is not scared or too upset about your mistake to leave you.

No matter what you are going through today, never forget that God is right there with you. He is faithful and will never abandon you. He's kinda awesome when it comes to stuff like this! He will always take care of you! No matter what!

KID PRAYER

. . . .

God, when I don't understand the tough stuff in life, help me trust and hold on to You. I know You have awesome things in my future and You love me.

PARENT PRAYER

. . . .

God, you will never give up on me, and I will never give up on You! Help me to not give in to fear and live life courageously!

YOU'RE GONNA REGRET THAT!!!

**Do not repay evil with evil or insult with insult.
On the contrary, repay evil with blessing, because to this
you were called so that you may inherit a blessing.**
1 Peter 3:9 (NIV)

Let's jump right in with a question today: When someone hurts your feelings, what is the first thought you have? Do you think, *Those people are so mean!* Why don't you take a minute to think about it. Think about a recent situation where your feelings got hurt by someone.

Do you have one in mind? While you are thinking about the situation, ask yourself these questions...

Did they mean to hurt your feelings? Were you having a bad day? Were they having a bad day? Were you in a bad mood? Or did something else happen to you earlier in the day, and you were already mad?

The reason why it's so important to ask yourself these questions before responding is because you might realize you aren't mad at them at all. Or you might realize they didn't mean to hurt your feelings in the first place.

It's true, you cannot control what people say or do to you, but you can control how you respond. If someone is being really mean to you, and you respond with kindness—or not at all—you may be surprised to learn that stuff like that doesn't even bother you as much. And the better you respond, the more you'll get along with others...and not regret (which means *you wish you would have never done it*) the things you say!

KID PRAYER

. . . .

God, I cannot control what others do, but I can control what I do. Give me the patience to think first and then respond—or to not respond at all.

PARENT PRAYER

. . . .

God, help me to know that I am not responsible for someone else's happiness. If someone hurts my feelings, I will extend Your grace to them and refuse to be offended.

I'M SO THIRSTY!

**Satisfy us in the morning with your unfailing love,
that we may sing for joy and be glad all our days.**
Psalm 90:14 (NIV)

Have you ever been outside on a warm summer day, running around, jumping through sprinklers, tossing water balloons, and then out of nowhere you realized you were **super-thirsty?** Like **so thirsty!** In that moment, all you can think about is taking a drink. And when you do, it tastes like the best drink ever. It takes the feeling of being thirsty and completely erases it. You can go back to whatever you were doing because you feel 100 percent back to full strength.

But here's a little tip: Start your day at 100 percent and stay there! How do you do that? You make a choice first thing in the morning to connect with God by saying, "God, Your love for me never fails and I'm totally happy in You." Just like we get thirsty for water on a hot day, we get really thirsty for God, too! Who knows, it might just make you so happy that you'll bust out in song. And do it every single day. Every single morning, you will have set yourself up for the best life in God.

KID PRAYER

. . . .

God, each morning let me say out loud how much You love me and that I am completely happy in You.

PARENT PRAYER

. . . .

God, You are my portion and You fully satisfy me. I am at my best as a parent when I am found in You.

WHAT WOULD YOU SAY?!

**Whoever restrains his words has knowledge,
and he who has a cool spirit is a man of understanding.**
Proverbs 17:27

· ·

You are the only one who can choose which words come out of your mouth. Yep! It's true. No one makes you say anything. If you feel like yelling, you can yell. If you want to be quiet, you close your mouth and don't say a peep. So, the lesson is this: You'll eventually have to say something in your life. You will eventually have to speak. The question is, what will you say?

Do you use words that hurt people? Or do you use words that make people feel better? Do you talk nicely to those around you? Or are you sometimes grumpy and use words that are a little unkind?

Here is the promise given to you *if* you choose words that sound most like God: He will bless you. And when God blesses you, it means He fully takes care of you. So, let God's words become your words and it will always work out for your good!

And who knows?! Unkind people may hear you speak and be so encouraged that they will start acting better themselves! They will hear how you talk and think, *Wow, that's a better way to live—better words to use.* It could be the thing that helps them realize they, too, need to start choosing their words better.

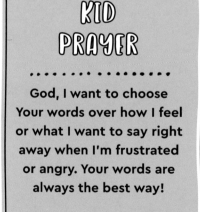

KID PRAYER

. . . .

God, I want to choose Your words over how I feel or what I want to say right away when I'm frustrated or angry. Your words are always the best way!

PARENT PRAYER

. . . .

God, help me to see that my words have power today, as well as power for tomorrow. Help me choose my words based on Your Word.

DON'T BLOW YOUR LID!

**Be angry and do not sin; do not let the
sun go down on your anger.**
Ephesians 4:26

Maybe you've experienced this before. It's cold outside and your mom or dad decides to make you a hot chocolate. They add the water to a pot or kettle and then crank up the heat to make the water boil. If you stand around in the kitchen and watch for the water to boil, it may feel like you are standing there forever!

You know why? It takes time for cold water to get hot. And it takes even more time for hot water to boil. This is similar to what happens when you get mad. You might not be a person who gets angry really easily or quickly, but not talking about things that bother you could be like a teapot getting hotter.

Over time, you start to get angry, and by the end, you just blow! But rather than ignore those feelings (which means *to not pay attention to them*) and explode at some point, the best choice you can make is to deal with your frustration right away.

Anger can be easy when it's little, but once it starts to boil, you'll have a hard time handling it. Think about it: Can you grab something super-hot off the stove? No way! It would hurt you. Anger is just like this: It's dangerous to let it get too hot...so cool it down and learn how to express your anger to God. Ask Him to help you deal with it and avoid blowing up!

KID PRAYER

God, I want to be patient and slow to respond...even when I'm angry or upset. But I need Your help and cannot do it on my own.

PARENT PRAYER

God, rather than get angry and lose my temper, I will quiet my mind, ask You for help and respond the way You would.

SAY NO TO FEAR

**You are my hiding place and my shield;
I hope in Your word.**
Psalm 119:114

God is your source of protection. When you are scared, feel hopeless, or like you have no one to turn to, God is right there, no matter what you are going through. Big or small, if it's a concern to you, it's a concern to God. That's how much He cares for you!

And He's not just a great place to hide, but He is also your shield. Shields are kind of amazing. And back in the Bible days, shields protected you from head to toe! So, no matter what comes at you today, ask God to be your shield. The minute something comes at you, it will be immediately deflected (which means *quickly knocked to the side*).

How can God be your shield? How can you hide in God? By studying His Word and speaking what it says out loud! In fact, you've been doing it for a little bit now with this devotional. Every time something comes against you, when it makes you feel small and not good enough, you run to God and say to that situation, "I am more than a conqueror in Christ Jesus!" (which means *you've got God and you've got this!*) You'll be amazed at how quickly you'll feel better!

KID PRAYER

. . . .

God, help me to run to You when I feel afraid. I know You will protect me.

PARENT PRAYER

. . . .

God, I choose to not place my hope in the things of this world, but solely in Your presence. You protect me when I feel overwhelmed and sustain me when I feel weak.

I'm not where I need to be, but thank God I'm not where I used to be either!

Because God is
on my side

I GET
BETTER+
BETTER

every day.

Philippians 1:6

THE CHOICE IS YOURS

I know what it is to be in need, and I know what it is
to have plenty. I have learned the secret of being content
in any and every situation, whether well fed or hungry,
whether living in plenty or in want.

Philippians 4:12 (NIV)

Quick question! How many choices have you already made today? You've probably picked out your clothes, helped your parents pack your lunch for school...you've made lots of choices! But have you made the choice about which attitude you will have today? Have you decided to have a good attitude or a bad one?

I know it sounds a little silly since you can't actually see an attitude, but it's a super-important thing to do before you start your day. And choosing to have a good one is one of the most incredible choices you'll make today. In fact, if you haven't done it, why don't you give it a try now? Ask God to give you a good attitude—and refuse to pick up a bad one.

You'd be surprised how something so simple can change the course of your day. Remember, do everything you can to ask God to help you with your day—and because He's good and loves to help you, He will always do it!

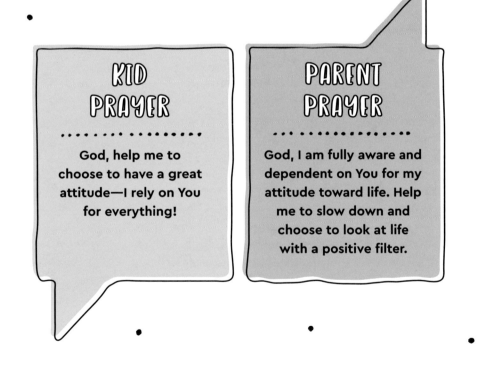

KID PRAYER

. . . .

God, help me to choose to have a great attitude—I rely on You for everything!

PARENT PRAYER

. . . .

God, I am fully aware and dependent on You for my attitude toward life. Help me to slow down and choose to look at life with a positive filter.

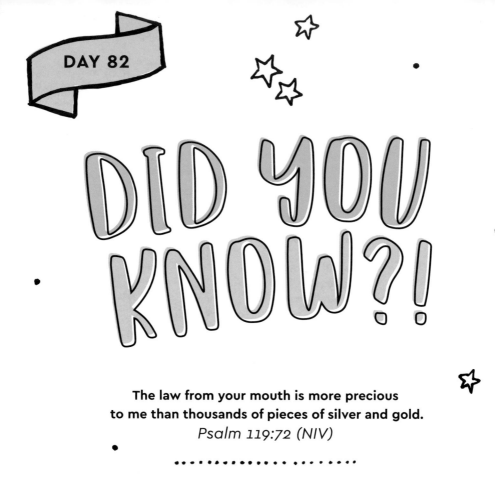

DID YOU KNOW?!

**The law from your mouth is more precious
to me than thousands of pieces of silver and gold.**
Psalm 119:72 (NIV)

. . . .

Did you know that God's Word is worth more than millions?
It's true. It's so valuable because it has the answer to every question in life. Just think about that! There's not one thing you'll face today that God's Word cannot help you with.

If you are having trouble getting along with your friends, you can read God's Word on the topic of relationships. If you are worried about a big test that's coming up, look up scriptures on fear and anxiety. If you want to know more about everything and anything, study God's Word on the topic of wisdom.

As you get older, you'll realize it's not "things" that make you happy anyway! There's nothing wrong with having stuff (gaming systems, tablets and things like that), but stuff isn't what keeps us happy—it's the joy we receive from God's Word that does!

KID PRAYER

. . . .

God, help me to be content and happy with all the many blessings You've given me. Rather than complain about what I don't have, I will be grateful for what I *do* have—especially Your Word!

PARENT PRAYER

. . . .

God, though I work hard to provide for my kids, I know that teaching them Your ways is the most important thing I could ever do for them.

I'LL NEVER GET IT

**But he said to me, "My grace is sufficient for you,
for my power is made perfect in weakness." Therefore
I will boast all the more gladly of my weaknesses, so that the
power of Christ may rest upon me.**
2 Corinthians 12:9

Do you remember the day you learned to ride your bike? Were you scared? Did you think you would instantly fall over and scrape your knee? You might have even yelled, "I can't do it! I don't know how—I'll **never** get it." It wasn't that you couldn't do it, but you were learning something new and that takes time.

But just when you were ready to give up, your mom or dad set you up as stable as possible and said to you, "You've got

this—you can do it!" You held on to the handlebars as tightly as possible, looked down the sidewalk and started peddling **super-fast!** Maybe you got it on the first try or maybe you didn't, but every time you fell, you learned what **not** to do.

You learn by failing at first. You get your balance when you overcome the wobbly feeling. You learn stability (which means *nothing can knock you down*) through those shaky feelings.

The same is true with God. It's when you're super-tired that God makes you strong. He teaches you how to be stable in His love—how to be confident even though you don't always get it right. Like a loving father or mother, God is always with you making everything less shaky and wobbly.

KID PRAYER

. . . .

God, I don't have to run away when I don't feel strong because You've promised me that if I say I need You, You will give me the strength.

PARENT PRAYER

. . . .

God, when I feel weak, when I doubt myself, I will choose to believe that You will help me with everything I need to do.

YOUR TEARS ARE IMPORTANT

**You have taken account of my wanderings;
Put my tears in Your bottle. Are they
not recorded in Your book?**
Psalm 56:8 (AMP)

Take a second to think about a time you've been sad or mad or upset. If you squeezed out a single tear or a lot of them, God has saved all of them! God is always with you, even though you can't see Him. He helps you when you are nervous or scared, and He is there to comfort you! He sees all the tears you cry.

You are so precious (which means *worth more than all the money in the world times a zillion*) to Him, and the things that make you sad are also important to Him. Think about it: You

belong to God; He loves you. When you are having a hard time, He is right there with you. So, why does He save your tears?

One reason is pretty simple: You mean a lot to Him, and so your tears mean a lot to Him! Here's another cool reason: If a friend had to catch all your tears, it means they would have to be close enough to you to do it. They couldn't be far away, and they would need to be with you at all times as tears can be tricky—they can show up at any time!

So, here's the point: Every time you feel sad, lonely or abandoned (which means *left all on your own*) and tears pour from your eyes, remember God is right there catching every last one of them.

KID PRAYER

· · · · · · · · · · · · · · ·

God, help me
to understand that
my tears matter to You.
Thank You for always
being close to me when
I am sad or lonely.

PARENT PRAYER

· · · · · · · · · · · · · · ·

God, even in the
tough moments of
life—I'm grateful You
are always with me.
And every concern I
have are concerns that
You are able to handle
and take care of.
I trust You!

WHAT DOES GOD SAY ABOUT YOU?

O Lord, you have searched me and known me! You know when I sit down and when I rise up; you discern my thoughts from afar. You search out my path and my lying down and are acquainted with all my ways.

Psalm 139:1-3

God has a lot to say about you. Yes, you...the wonderful and unique person you are. And because He created you, it's good to remind yourself of what God thinks about you.

You mean everything to God! When He made you, He breathed His breath into your body, and then you began to breathe. Before you were even a teeny, tiny baby in your mom's belly, God knew you and was already planning great things for your life.

Not only does He know how many hairs are on your head, He also knows every single word you will say and everything you'll do in your life. So, when you start feeling sad about the things you're not good at, remember that God created you— you are His kid! And for the one or two things you're not good at, He has twenty more things that you **are** good at!

He loves you, and He loves to be with you!

KID PRAYER
· · · · · · · · · · · · · ·

God, help me fully see and understand how much You love me.

PARENT PRAYER
· · · · · · · · · · · · · · · ·

God, help me to say goodbye to stress, anxiety and worry because I know You know everything about me and my kids. Your love for us both is endless, and I will rest in that.

MONKEY BARS

**I have fought the good fight, I have
finished the race, I have kept the faith.**
2 Timothy 4:7

· · · · · · · · · · · · · · · · · · · ·

When you were little, you watched as all the other kids swung across the bars on the playground. Everyone told you, "You are too little for the monkey bars! If you try them, you'll get hurt!" And though at first that was true, now you're older. You're taller. You are **stronger** than you were when you were little.

One day, you got to the playground and decided that today was the day! You were going to **do** the monkey bars! And not just do them, but you were going to make it **all** the way across. So, you jumped up on the platform and grabbed the first bar as tightly as you could. You swung out and as you were floating above the ground, you were filled with excitement and a little bit of fear. You thought to yourself, *Can I **really** make it all the way across?*

And though you could have easily gone back to the safety of the platform, you had made up your mind that you would keep going. You persevered. You kept at it. Even though with each bar you grabbed it got harder and harder to keep holding on, you focused on the end—on the other side of the platform.

In your life, you will have different moments where you have to decide if you should give up or not, but don't even waste your time! God is ready to send you His strength, stamina (which means *the energy to keep going*) and focus...all you have to do is ask for it. You've got this!

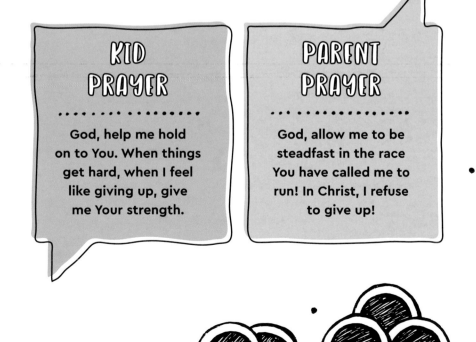

KID PRAYER

God, help me hold on to You. When things get hard, when I feel like giving up, give me Your strength.

PARENT PRAYER

God, allow me to be steadfast in the race You have called me to run! In Christ, I refuse to give up!

DID YOU KNOW?!

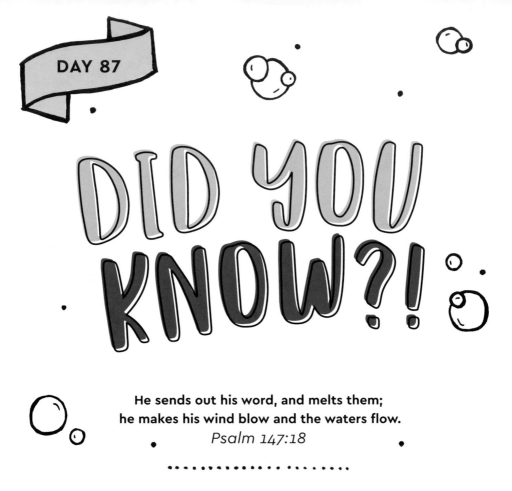

**He sends out his word, and melts them;
he makes his wind blow and the waters flow.**
Psalm 147:18

Did you know that God is the one who melts the ice and snow? Whether you live where it snows a lot or not at all, God's Word says He warms the earth and ice and snow turn back to water. That's amazing! But the ice and snow of winter aren't the only super-cold things sometimes.

Sometimes, your heart can be cold and feel like it's frozen. That sounds odd doesn't it? How in the world does your heart feel snowy? What makes it that way?

Well, you may not know this, but during winter, the earth is a little more tilted (which means *it's more on its side*). And that means the sun's rays don't hit it with as much power! Plus, the days are shorter and it gets dark pretty early. You combine those two things and you've got winter!

Does your life feel a little tilted? Do you feel like you haven't had enough direct contact with God? That you haven't talked to Him in a while? Have you put yourself in direct contact with His light?

If you're feeling cold today (which means *you have an "I don't care" attitude about stuff*), ask God to warm and thaw your heart. The best first move? Lean and tilt into Him as close as you can.

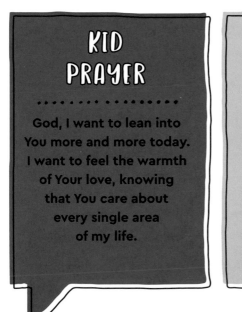

KID PRAYER

God, I want to lean into You more and more today. I want to feel the warmth of Your love, knowing that You care about every single area of my life.

PARENT PRAYER

God, instead of choosing the path of self-effort and self-strength, I will lean into the warmth of Your heart and allow You to instill in me my sense of worth and value as Your child.

THE END IS REALLY JUST A NEW BEGINNING!

Do not be conformed to this world, but be transformed by the renewal of your mind....
Romans 12:2

Saying goodbye to anything is always tough! Whether the school year is coming to an end, or you are watching a movie you love and it's almost over. Or maybe it's the end of something that is really hard to say goodbye to. But the good news is—no matter what—an end is really just the start to a new beginning.

Perhaps someone you've been friends with no longer wants to be friends with you. Maybe your best friend moved out of state and you miss them! In the moment, it does seem sad, and that's okay. But the feelings of sadness or loneliness won't last forever. Even if that sounds impossible for you to believe right now, God loves you too much to let you be sad or lonely forever.

Instead, know that because God loves you, He wants you to be open (which means *to be willing*) to something new and great coming into your life. Sadness is never fun, but the hope of something great is fun! And that's God's promise to you. He wants you to have a great life.

So how does God do this for you? Simple. He comes right where you are, in the very moment where you feel things are at an end, and He says, "I'm here with you, and I've got a lot of great things ahead for you!"

KID PRAYER

God, help me be excited and have a good attitude about new adventures and new possibilities!

PARENT PRAYER

God, as my children encounter new situations, help me to confidently support and encourage them to give it their best, and always point them back to You!

AN ADVENTURE IN THE WOODS

Show me your ways, Lord, teach me your paths. Guide me in your truth and teach me, for you are God my Savior, and my hope is in you all day long.

Psalm 25:4-5 (NIV)

Have you ever gone on an adventure or explored the woods around your house? Well, whether you have or you haven't, how about you go on one right now—in your imagination!

First, imagine you are looking at the opening of a semi-hidden trail. Your first thought is, *That looks a little scary.* But you've already learned how to **do it afraid**, so you get closer and closer to the opening and decide to poke your head into the clearing...

And when you do, it's like you discover a secret door to somewhere awesome! And once inside, everything opens up. There is a twisting path, birds are chirping and cheering you on, and all you want to do is run! Though you were a little afraid standing on the outside, now that you are inside, you feel like you can take on anything!

You start with careful steps, but after a minute or so, you find yourself running down the path. Like a drum that's keeping time as each foot slams onto the ground, you race through the woods because you are excited about where the path will take you.

And just like the excitement of racing down a secret path in the woods, it's a great reminder that your life in Jesus is an adventure. Sure, you may not always do everything right, but if you keep one foot in front of the other, God will always take care of you and it will be thrilling!

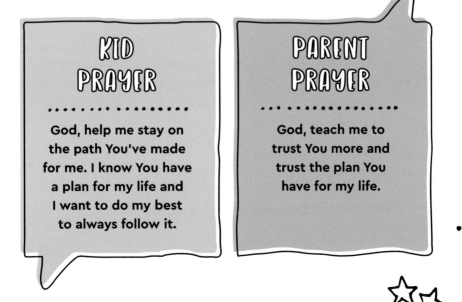

KID PRAYER

. . . .

God, help me stay on the path You've made for me. I know You have a plan for my life and I want to do my best to always follow it.

PARENT PRAYER

. . . .

God, teach me to trust You more and trust the plan You have for my life.

DAY 90

JUST SAY NO!

"Judge not, and you will not be judged...."
Luke 6:37

• •

It's hard to keep your mouth closed when you see something you don't agree with or that you don't like. You might be walking down the street and see someone wearing something you think looks funny, and it's easy to judge them based on what they're wearing.

You might be in a conversation today with a friend and they might talk about some of their family traditions. Their family might not go see certain movies or they don't eat certain foods. They might do things that seem different or wrong in your eyes, but don't give in to the temptation to judge them!

Remember, God made **you** an individual and He made **them** individuals. The decisions they make are between them and God. God will take care of them, so you only need to think about the things you are choosing. The best way to live—the way that will bring you the most peace—is without any judgment! Love people like Jesus does!

KID PRAYER

God, help me to support others and to look at them the way You do—without judgment!

PARENT PRAYER

God, help me to not judge others for the way they parent or live their life. They are doing the best they can, and I will do the same for what works best for my family.

With God, I'm better than I was yesterday, and I know my

BEST

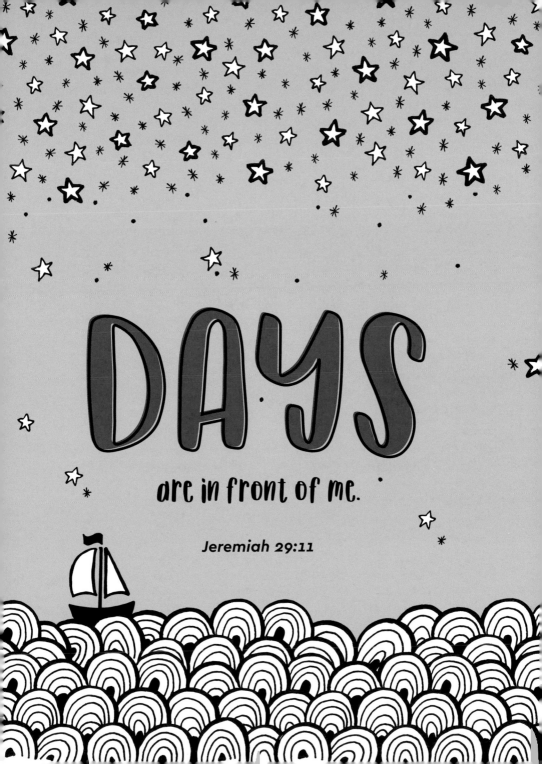

DAYS

are in front of me.

Jeremiah 29:11

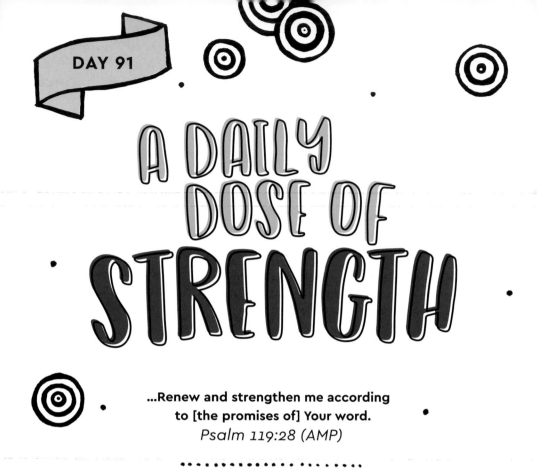

A DAILY DOSE OF STRENGTH

> ...Renew and strengthen me according
> to [the promises of] Your word.
> *Psalm 119:28 (AMP)*

God is the one who gives you strength! That's right. Even this morning when you woke up and you just wanted to pull the covers over your head, God was preparing (which means *getting you ready for*) every ounce of strength you'd need. Even if you don't immediately feel strong, God's strength is waiting for you.

And every single morning, whether you've gotten enough sleep or not, God will always send you a new batch of

strength for all the things you'll face today. It is His unending promise to you.

So, you **are** strong today! You **can** take on anything that comes your way! There is nothing that can overwhelm God's strength, so you've already got an edge. You serve the God of the universe, and He loves you and is setting you up to have one incredible day!

KID PRAYER

God, help me to be strong today—no matter what's coming!

PARENT PRAYER

God, send endless amounts of comfort and strength my way. They will be the things that keep me going.

ARE WE THERE YET?

For as he thinks in his heart, so is he...
Proverbs 23:7 (AMP)

. . . .

Go ahead and read those four words above out loud with your best whining voice! **Are. We. Thhhhhhhheeere. YET?**

You've said this before, haven't you? On a long road trip, you end up sitting for hours and hours. And though you do your best to be patient, you eventually end up **totally** bored! And after an hour of that total boredom, you yell to the front, *"Are we there yet?!"*

You may even have moments where you want to scream it out, but you know where that leads—big trouble from the parents! So, you try to be patient and hold it together, but it's all you can think about!

But is that the **only** thing you can think about? Or could you be more creative with your thoughts while you wait to get there? It's true that these thoughts won't make the three hours left of the ride magically disappear, but focusing on the irritation, annoyance and anger won't help either. In fact, focusing on those thoughts will only make the ride seem longer.

And though it may not have wheels like the car does, your mind is like a vehicle, and I often say, "Where you let your mind go, the rest of you will follow." If you want to travel down the road to anger, irritation and frustration, it will certainly take you there. But if you want to travel to peace, patience and joy, make your mind up and think about those things. It sure will make the car ride more fun!

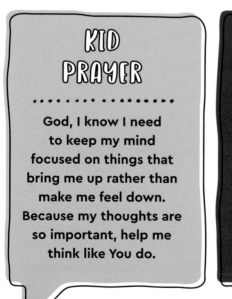

KID PRAYER

God, I know I need to keep my mind focused on things that bring me up rather than make me feel down. Because my thoughts are so important, help me think like You do.

PARENT PRAYER

God, when I get caught up in all the negative thoughts of this world, it makes me weak and feel defeated. Instead, help me meditate on the goodness of Your Word.

OUCH! THAT SOUP IS BLAZING HOT!

**Blessed is the one who finds wisdom,
and the one who gets understanding.**
Proverbs 3:13

. . . .

Have you ever gone to your grandma's house or a friend's house and they've made fresh soup or chili? Imagine that it's a cold day, it's kind of dark and dreary outside, and so you're in your comfy clothes. You grab a bowl and a spoon, head to the table with all the extra stuff (cheese, sour cream, onions... yes, even those!) with your steaming hot bowl of fresh chili.

Now, what's the next best thing to do? You sit down, check. You grab some cheese; maybe some sour cream; and if you're extra brave, a couple onions...check. And as steam is rising off the top, do you take a big spoonful and pop it in your mouth? No way!

And why would that be a terrible thing to do? Did you say, "Because it's too hot and will burn you?!" Yes! You are right.

Sometimes you have to use both wisdom and patience before doing something—even something good like eating a tasty bowl of chili! If you jump into something too soon, you may find out that it doesn't work out. If you don't ask God to help you with those decisions, you may find yourself in a blazing hot situation where all you want to do is jump right back out!

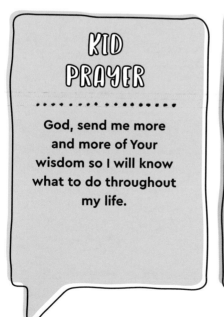

KID PRAYER

God, send me more and more of Your wisdom so I will know what to do throughout my life.

PARENT PRAYER

God, send me all the wisdom I need to navigate this life with my kids. I may not immediately know the right decision, but show me the best decision as I quiet myself to hear it.

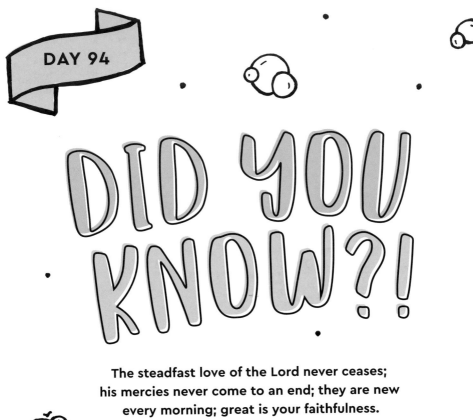

DID YOU KNOW?!

**The steadfast love of the Lord never ceases;
his mercies never come to an end; they are new
every morning; great is your faithfulness.**
Lamentations 3:22-23

Every single day, God gives you a new batch of mercy. Did you wake up this morning upset or bothered by what happened yesterday? Are you still thinking about all the ways you messed up? Here's an even more important question: Have you asked God for forgiveness? Have you made it right with Him? If not, before your feet hit the ground, take the time to ask Him for mercy!

God is so good at coming through on His promises, and this is one of His best. Think about it like this: Every day you get to hit the reset button. Which means, no matter what's happened, God says, "Take a do-over! I have new mercy for you." Were you rude to your parents? Did you cheat on a test? Did you break a promise?

Well guess what? As long as you take the time to make it right and talk to God, He says He will give you mercy and you can start over (*in fact, that's what mercy means!*). That's something to be very excited about! And it's the best way to get your day started!

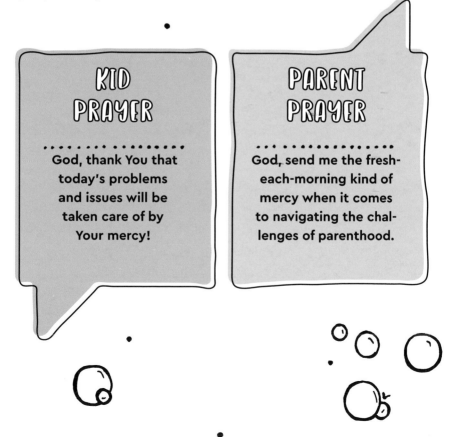

KID PRAYER

God, thank You that today's problems and issues will be taken care of by Your mercy!

PARENT PRAYER

God, send me the fresh-each-morning kind of mercy when it comes to navigating the challenges of parenthood.

GET IN THE GAME!

**I say to myself, "The Lord is my portion;
therefore I will wait for him."**
Lamentations 3:24 (NIV)

Have you ever had family game night or sat around a table with a bunch of friends at a party? You know how it goes. The games get laid out on the table and everyone starts deciding which one to play. Some are fast, and some make you think really hard. But no matter what, the point of playing a game is to win. And it's not just you who wants to win—*everyone* wants to win—that's what seems to be the most important thing!

And though there is nothing wrong with beating all your friends and being good at a game...**real life** is **not** always like that. Life isn't about **winning** all the time. Sure, at first it sounds crazy, but the number one thing you can do is to live for God with everything you have.

What's more important than winning? Doing the right thing and doing whatever God asks you to do. That may mean you let your friends go first in line or be willing to not get your way. But when you trust God with your life and focus on doing things His way, you'll win in the best way possible—in God's eyes!

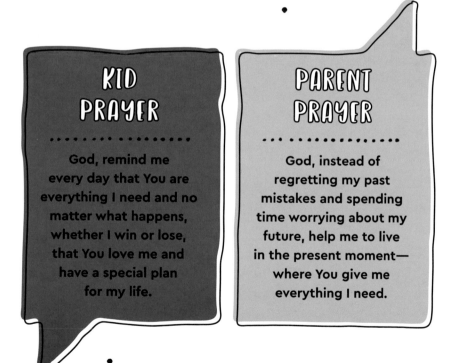

KID PRAYER

God, remind me every day that You are everything I need and no matter what happens, whether I win or lose, that You love me and have a special plan for my life.

PARENT PRAYER

God, instead of regretting my past mistakes and spending time worrying about my future, help me to live in the present moment— where You give me everything I need.

DAY 96

GOD'S GOT YOU!

The Lord watches over you....
Psalm 121:5 (NIV)

Never forget this powerful truth: God always keeps His eye on you. When you are sleeping, He makes sure to watch over you, so you can get good rest. When you wake up, He's happy to say, "Good morning!" As you go through your day, He's there every step of the way.

Does it mean everything is always awesome? Does it mean that everything in your life is always great? No. Sadly, we do live in a world where bad things might happen, but God is not bad and does not cause the bad things. It's quite the opposite!

Though life can be hard sometimes, your relationship with God can help you get through those moments—and—you can come out on the other end better than you were before!

And He does all of it because He cares for you. In fact, take the amount of love your parents have for you and multiply it by a zillion. His love for you has no limits. When you feel like nobody understands you, God does. When you feel like you are sad and alone and that there's nothing to be happy about, God calls out to you, "Hey! We have each other. There will never be a moment I'm not with you!"

So, if today you are super-happy, super-sad, super-lonely or maybe just super-duper okay, know that God sees you and will continue to take care of you.

KID PRAYER

God, even when bad things happen, remind me daily that You are watching over me and help me to see more of You in everything I do.

PARENT PRAYER

God, even when things don't go how I want, You are with me exactly where I am. Thank You for being with me in the middle of my great moments and not-so-great moments.

TIME FOR CHORES!

**For we aim at what is honorable not only in the
Lord's sight but also in the sight of man.**
2 Corinthians 8:21

• •

After a long week of school, you wake up on a bright and sunny Saturday morning! You get dressed and race to the front door. And at the very moment your hand hits the handle, your mom or dad yells out, "Did you finish your chores?" [*Gulp*]

"Chores?" Ugh. You think to yourself, *No, no I didn't do my chores! But it's just taking out the trash and bringing my dirty clothes down...and that's something I can do anytime. It's Saturday! And all my friends are going to be outside in the street and I don't want to miss out on anything. I want to have fun and all of that stuff can wait.*

And then, from out of nowhere, you have this interesting thought: *If I pretend I didn't hear my parents, and if I pretend my chores are done, I can keep going.*

You know what you **should** do, but it's not what you **want** to do. And I remember the day God taught me this lesson: *Wisdom means doing now what you will be happy with later on!*

Though making the right decision isn't always **easy to do**, it's always the **right thing to do**. In fact, making the right decision to turn around and do the chores now will actually help you later when you're outside having a blast with friends. You won't be focused on other things while you are playing and can have that sunny Saturday you've been waiting for!

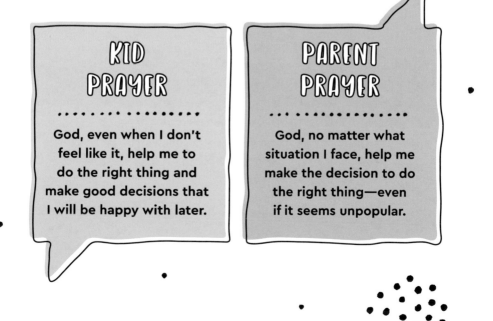

KID PRAYER

God, even when I don't feel like it, help me to do the right thing and make good decisions that I will be happy with later.

PARENT PRAYER

God, no matter what situation I face, help me make the decision to do the right thing—even if it seems unpopular.

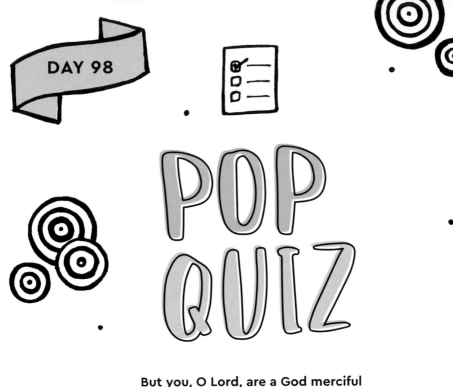

POP QUIZ

**But you, O Lord, are a God merciful
and gracious, slow to anger and abounding
in steadfast love and faithfulness.**

Psalm 86:15

You get to school in the morning and you expect the day to be like every other day at school. You go over math, continuing to learn how to subtract and carry. In social studies, you learn as many of the states and capitals as possible. In writing, you brush up on all the different parts of speech.

But then something different happens! When you get back to your desk after lunch, your teacher announces, "Okay guys

and girls, it's time for a quick pop quiz..." At that moment, do you feel a little queasy?

She starts asking questions and you get nervous and start guessing. You do your best, but as she reads off the answers after the quiz is over, you realize you've missed half of them. What does it mean? You know exactly what that means...you just got an F on the quiz.

But don't be angry with yourself! Sometimes things like this happen. Sure, you wish you had done a better job—got a better grade—but the grade is not who you are. So, cut yourself some slack (which means *to be easy on yourself*) and keep moving. Don't stay stuck in this moment. You know you'll do better next time, and this little pop quiz will only help you focus better as you move forward.

KID PRAYER

. . . .

God, thank You for being slow to get angry. When I feel like I've failed, help me to be slow to get angry at myself.

PARENT PRAYER

. . . .

God, when I am frustrated, when I feel like I'm at my wit's end, allow me to respond with Your loving kindness instead of quick anger.

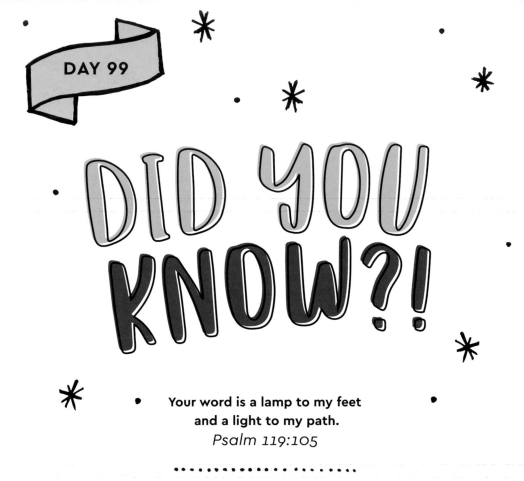

DID YOU KNOW?!

**Your word is a lamp to my feet
and a light to my path.**
Psalm 119:105

Did you know God's Word lights up everything around you?
Even if everything seems dark. Even when you aren't sure
which way to go, look to God's Word. God has a plan and a
path for your life. Before you were even born, God was busy
clearing the path ahead of you. He knows exactly what you
need and when you need it.

God is also active (which means *He is always moving*) in
all the people in your life, too! He wants you to have good

friends and great relationships! That doesn't mean the path is always going to be easy—that you won't deal with tough times. But, it means as long as you keep close to God and His Word, the path will always be underneath your feet.

So, next time your life feels shaky, rather than just deal with it, jump into God's Word. Ask Him to help you. And like the light of a flashlight being switched on in a dark room, His Word pushes back all the darkness, and you can see everything more clearly!

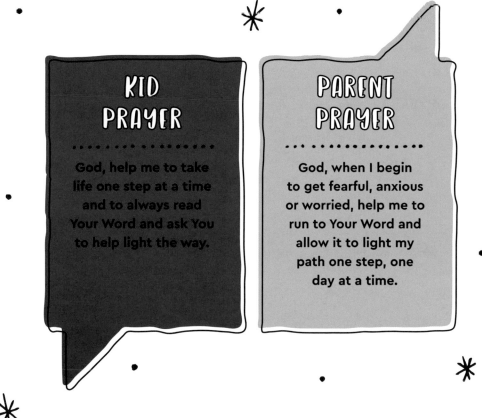

KID PRAYER

God, help me to take life one step at a time and to always read Your Word and ask You to help light the way.

PARENT PRAYER

God, when I begin to get fearful, anxious or worried, help me to run to Your Word and allow it to light my path one step, one day at a time.

WARM SUMMER NIGHT'S DRIVE

**Casting all your cares [all your anxieties,
all your worries, and all your concerns, once and
for all] on Him, for He cares about you....**
1 Peter 5:7 (AMP)

• •

Summer is *one* of the best times of the year! The reason? There's a lot of time with friends and family and moments where you can just go with the flow and do fun stuff. Maybe you've had an experience like this...

On a warm summer's day, you hear your mom or dad yell out, "Come on! We're going for a drive! Let's jump in the car, roll down all the windows and just drive!"

As you sit in your seat, you watch as trees and buildings pass by. You hold your hand out and pretend it's a rollercoaster car as it rises and falls in the breeze. And then, you find yourself breathing easier—enjoying the moment. You aren't thinking of anything, but you are simply along for the ride.

With God, you can learn how to go with the flow and enjoy your day no matter how it might look or how you might feel. The Bible uses the phrase "cast your cares" and what it means is this: You can hop in the car of life with God, feel the warm summer's night air in your face and simply rest in Him. He wants you to learn how to enjoy your life and relax in Him.

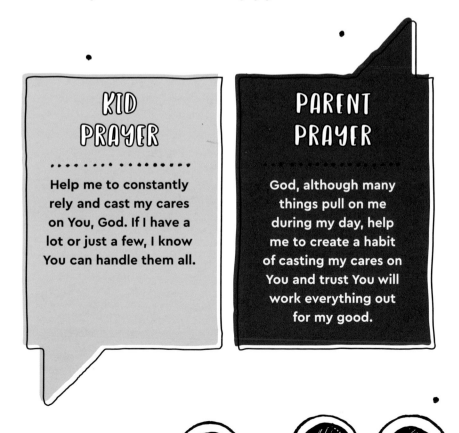

KID PRAYER

Help me to constantly rely and cast my cares on You, God. If I have a lot or just a few, I know You can handle them all.

PARENT PRAYER

God, although many things pull on me during my day, help me to create a habit of casting my cares on You and trust You will work everything out for my good.

ARE WE READY FOR THIS?

And I am sure of this, that he who began a good work in you will bring it to completion at the day of Jesus Christ.
Philippians 1:6

It's hard to believe that about 101 days ago, you picked up this book and started learning more about God and yourself! It might have been super-hot outside when you started or freezing cold. You may have even been another age or grown two or three inches. No matter what, it shows that you are constantly growing!

No matter what happens, if it's been the ***best day ever*** for 101 days or you've had some tough moments along the way, you are always given a fresh start—**a new day**. God loves you so much that He's going to stick with you for the **next** 101 and the next 101! And I often remind myself of this idea: I may not be where I need to be, but thank God I'm not where I used to be. I'm okay and I'm on my way!

And because God wants to see you live the good life He's designed for you, you have one more piece of homework, one more thing you have to do as you end this devotional: You must stand up wherever you are, get your parents to join you, and do the following last thing...

At the top of your lungs, yell as loud as you can: "I am never going to give up! I know that God loves me, and I will never stop learning more about Him!"

KID PRAYER

God, thank You for always sticking with me. Help me to never give up and always know that You are leading me and will help me have the *best day ever.*

PARENT PRAYER

God, help me to constantly remind my kids of Your unfailing love. And not just for them, but to know that Your grace extends to me and in You, I can be the *Best. Parent. Ever.*